God's Wisdom

God's Wisdom

Jemela Mwelu

Fivefeetnine Productions
Bronx, New York
2014

Books by Jemela Mwelu

Reclaiming Heaven

*A Collection of Poetry, Essays,
Short Stories, and Meditations*

This book was printed in the United States of America.

ISBN: Softcover 0-9785345-1-4
ISBN 13: 9780978534516

Cover art and design: Neal Izumi, nizumi@mac.com
Author Photo: jon@jonathanconklin.net

Published by Fivefeetnine Productions
Bronx, New York
www.fivefeetnine.com

**To order additional copies of this book contact: www.createspace.
com/4511326, www.amazon.com/dp/0978534514, or other retail outlets**

In memory of Paramahansa Yogananda and
Joel S. Goldsmith for their vital contribution
to the spiritual wakening of humanity.

Blessings for Eckhart Tolle to continue
his mission to make us aware of the
importance of living in the NOW.

∽◯

"There is no God out here in space. The God there is, is
hidden within us, waiting for each one of us to discover for
himself. We do not have to go any place in time or space.
The spiritual journey, the greatest of all adventures, is not
made in time or space. It is a journey in consciousness—
and this journey no one can make for us."

A Parenthesis in Eternity
Joel S. Goldsmith

Author's Note

God asked me to acknowledge three things before I started this book.

1. Respect for the work I give you
2. Discipline to follow through
3. Growth to grow your soul

I pray I have been obedient to his requests.

Psalm 45:1 Prayer for deliverance

My heart is inditing a good matter: I speak of things which I have made touching the king: my tongue is the pen of a ready writer.

Contents

Question

If there is nothing new under the sun, the question to man is can the beginning of anything ever be found? If so, where is it and where is its home?

Introduction

I LOVE WHEN GOD TALKS TO ME

I love you Father/Mother/God.
I hear you speaking to me, through me.
I am filled to the brim with light and love.
I could be traveling on a congested highway
or at a concert in Madison Square Garden,
and all becomes still when I hear
your greeting, "Hello, daughter."
I never long for Earth arms to hold me.
I never long for companionship.
I am never missing love, respect,
direction, and purpose for being.
I know I can hear my true
Father/Mother talking to me.
I am listening to what God wants me
to reflect to the world through him.

Jemela Mwelu

Face of God

To draw the face of God is to draw a self-portrait because *I AM*[1] you and live within you and *My* face has many faces of all colors, sizes, and shapes. *My* face can never be seen because all who have ever come to know *Me* meet *Me* in the invisible life.

---

1 The words "*My, Me*, and *I AM*" capitalized refer to God.

The Universal *I Am*

If *I AM* you
and You are *Me*
then We are Us
and Us are Them.

Ripple Effect

When you become love,
you become it for eternity.
You become a ripple effect
throughout the universe
for all eternity.

Mind vs. Matter

Mind over matter.
Mind over nothing.
Spirit governs all!

Magic

There is no magic.
Everything is made manifest
by *My* divine will
to express love for the world
and to sustain
all life that lives for eternity.

Truth

Truth is timeless.
It never, never experiences irrelevancy.

Mind

The mind has weakened man's faith because man is always looking for proof for every reason to believe; therefore, man's reality is in constant fluctuation. The mind of man refuses to accept that God *IS* and that should be enough. But the mind drives man to want to question why *I AM* who *I AM* and why I do not move and manifest things in man's *mind time*. *I AM* infinitely patient with this *proof mind process* man struggles with. I speak to man always. Sometimes I speak in a rainbow, earthquake, or a flood. Sometimes I fill a soul like vapor, filling them up with *My* presence so they feel they will burst with joy when their cup runneth over. I release *Myself* from them as tears. *I AM* always talking and walking with man. Those who have evolved to the place of surrender embrace this knowing and struggle, not with time, simply just work and do. The mind of man is both friend and foe. It is man's challenge to make peace with it and direct it to express nothing but love to all living things in creation.

Hear, Speak, and See

Hear no evil.
Speak no evil.
See no evil.
Why?
Because evil, like goodness,
is created by man's mind.
Speak love.
See love.
Be love.
Love is all.
Love is all *I* gave to man.
Love has always been
and will never cease to exist.

The mind creates the scale
of how much to love, to share
with one another.
My love is perfect balance.
My love can never be weighed.

Life

Life is eternal.
Everyone and everything
is recycled in the kingdom.

Formation of the Divine Trilogy

MIND

BODY

SPIRIT

The alignment is achieved by absence of negative thought.

Obedience begins the purge.

Purification is made manifest when
the *trilogy* is balanced and reflects
peace, harmony, and love.
Your continence is always reflected.

Sonship

Do you know *My* son?
Because if you do,
then you know
he and you are
one in the same.

Goal of the Writer

There is always the triumph of the human
spirit when he or she recognizes that God is within.
Every aspect of their true divine nature is the soul of God.

The Infinite Invisible

Everything is held together by thought.
Nothing is real.
The only thing that is real is the invisible.
There is always room
because thoughts continually dissolve.
As they dissolve,
so does the material manifestation
to make room for more thought creations.
There is no room that exists
in the infinite invisible.

What is the Soul?

The soul is the essence of free will until it is united to the divine, which is the spirit. It is all One united. Soul is the experience of *My* journey through human form. But man has been given free will to decide navigation. When man loses control of his navigation, then I will take control. Man must navigate his earth experiences to return to *Me* in spirit. All is One.

Obedience of the
Disciplined Soul

Obedience is the pathway
to inner understanding.
Without the practice of obedience
you perceive mixed messages.

The external world never
stops for pause or reflection.
It is always reflecting
what the massive collective consciousness of man is
thinking.
This is what a soul without obedience
is keyed into listening to.

An awakened soul knows
the difference
of where the information is being perceived from
and will act on the information
set forth from the world within *My* domain.

Obedience acted upon with love
is effortless.

No Mask

My face is seen through
the countenance of your being.
Everything *I AM* and exist
for is revealed through
obtaining Christ consciousness.

Christ was not the only powerful reflection
of *Me* I expressed to the world.
I showed *My* face to man
in many parts of the world
and through Buddha,
Mohamed, Quan Yin,
and countless others who
reached for enlightenment
to reflect *My* face to humanity.

I AM love only, pure and simple.
There is nothing more
that needs to be expressed.
If man looks around
with spiritual eyes
all *My* love can be seen
as expressed through
something as small as a seed
that keeps bringing forth food
and beauty with every blossoming season.

To wear *My* face
you must discover the mask
man hides behind from within.
Once the struggle of man thinks he really is realized,
then all is melted away from the mask.
My face can be revealed throughout eternity.

Ego is man's possession of expression.
I AM only One.
I and *I AM* all in One.
You cannot separate yourself from
the creator that made you.
I AM You and You are *Me*.

Blocking *My* Love

(Man: "If I'm not reflecting it, then I'm not it!")

Humankind is designed
to always be in a state
of receiving and giving love.

The brain or mind is the
operating system that
sends the signals
to the dense physical
to instruct the body
how to care for it
and keep it functioning
and aligned to do the earth work
of engaging other beings in one
universal accord…LOVE.

The human appearance
gives the illusion of many, but
there is only one universal soul.
My soul operates
through each and everyone
on the physical plane.
Deep within man is *My* center.
The journey is to find it

and reveal its true essence,
which is Love,
only pure Love.

The mind is a deceptive built-in feature.
Its only function
is to maintain balance
in all it makes manifest
from the invisible to the visible.

When the mind is attuned
to universal harmony and love,
the ONE is all that exists.
The experience of the earth life
is to figure out
how to return to the ONE.
The *I AM* ONE,
not the *I AM* individual self.

Too Many Questions

The questions are
questions that trigger
the return to the ONE.

The question regarding
human existence
begins to reveal
that all is spirit
and the spirit,
only the ONE
united spirit,
emanates from *Me*.

Ownership

There is no ownership.
Why?
Because everything is spirit
and it has no need
to store anything
once anything is actualized
and made manifest.

You can't take anything with you
when you return to the ONE.
You cannot preserve
anything in physical form.
Ashes to ashes
is necessary
to keep making room
for continual creation.

The Inner Voice

Many hear *Me* but turn away. *I AM* always talking to *My* creations. *I AM* always shining the light on the path they need to follow. But I have created man to possess free will. It is this free will that acts like a compass directing your feet on the divine path that eventually leads to *Me*, or the force of man's free will that makes choices that leads him or her in all sorts of detours. The life cycle is created in one big circle. There is no beginning or end. There are no corners or detours. The only detours that take place are those created by the human mind that tries to direct the soul. The mind can never, ever direct the soul. Why? Because *I AM* the only soul force that exists and I created the mind. Think of the Earth where you play hide-and-seek games. Everything is here for man. Nothing is hidden. The mind of man or the intellect of mind is constantly spinning and spinning in the earth life and constantly manifesting creations of the mind. However, when man learns to calm the mind, stop the detours, and seek calm and solitude, then he can hear *Me* speaking to him throughout eternity. There is not a he or she existence in the work I created; only spirit exists. The male and female expression is necessary for the reproduction system for *My* continual soul experience and expression on the Earth I created. I only speak in one voice. I only express myself in the invisible world, the real world. All can hear *Me* when they learn to drop the veil of trying to recreate through the mind what I have already given man in the spirit, which is made flesh.

Ecclesiastes or the "The Preacher"
Chapter 1:9

Thine that hath been, it is that which shall be; and that which is done: that which shall be done: and there is no new thing under the sun.

Wants and Needs

You ask *Me* for everything
I have already given you.
The mind has been used to
misstep into fantasy and desires
that only mind can create.
The soul knows the truth
and the direction to follow
the path home back to *Me*.
When the soul directs the mind,
abundance is clearly in view.
There is no shame
in the nakedness of the truth revealed.
Man is always asking
for things that are already available.
But the dilemma for man
is the insatiable appetite of the mind
to never be satisfied
because it always wants more.
The enlightened soul
sees the dilemma of the mind
and seeks nothing in the material world.
Why?
Because the soul provides all you need
and because I have already given you
everything you need.

Guidance

Everything I want you to know
is written in *My* voice and *My* words.
I have always placed teachers
among the masses
to remind them
that there is only one true source
of light and love.
That is *Me,*
and all who see *Me*
dwell within *Me*
for eternity.
The teacher prophets
apostles of the old world languages,
changes in names,
in man's time to sages, mystics,
seers, psychics, and fortunetellers.
The list of names man
has given *My* chosen messengers
and teachers are endless.
Man has forgotten the first
teacher I sent to the
Christian world
was *My* son Jesus.
I have sent others before *My* son
to the world,

but their assignments
were not as difficult as the task
I assigned to *My* son.
He was assigned to show man
that the spirit lives
beyond the flesh,
which was witnessed
by his resurrection.
He is proof
that all who believe in *Me*
have eternal life.
He revealed
there is no fear in death
as man knows death
through his dense
physical experience.
He or she when baptized
in the spirit of *My* son
has been reborn to the world
as a resurrected spirit
to do *My* work for the world.
Man was scattered
around the Earth,
divided by tongues
and geology of the Earth.
But the task
of man's universal mission
is to come together
on all parts of the Earth.
One soul united under *Me*

by love of all living things
big and small
and come to the realization
that ALL IS ONE
and that ALL is *Me*
reflecting in the world forever.

What is the Heart?

What is the heart
if not a tool for the soul to discern
the direction the soul should take?
Man has taken the meaning
of what the heart actually does
to manipulate fears and emotions
of their brothers and sisters.
If love is the ultimate goal
for the return to *Me,*
then why is the heart
used to judge the character of the being?

Love is total love
for everything I have created,
including man himself.

Love is neither male nor female.
It has nothing to do
with the tool of the heart.

When experiences are
emotionally imbalanced,
perceived by the mind
the experiences
automatically lodge in the heart.
The heart is the sensor

that monitors man's capability
to experience love.

When an emotion
enters the sensor,
the spirit has the power
to direct the emotion.

When man feels his mind
is more powerful than his soul,
the soul will idle
and let man run with his mind.

Because I have given man eternity
to return to *Me*,
the process of finding
the key to use the heart
for the function it is meant to serve
continues to perplex man
and delay his return
to the ONE *I AM*.

When man finally learns
that love is not individual, but universal,
encompassing all of creation,
then and only then is love actualized
and experienced by the soul.

You ask *Me* about man and woman love.
I make no distinction as to gender

for who will experience pure love,
which I have given man.

Spirit is *Me* and *I AM*
reflecting love
in everything and everyone.

Man's Law and *My* Love

❧

My laws are simple.
Love one another
and learn divine obedience.
When called upon to do thy will,
there are no deadlines
or consequences
for living in the light of love.

Man, on the other hand,
has used his mind to
manipulate and separate
the love that is so abundant
for the receiving and the giving.

Question is,
if I give
love to all mankind so freely,
why did *I* give man a mind
to use against his fellowman
to manipulate all I give man
so freely?

The answer is this.
The mind is a seed
planted in the soul of man.
If he learns to align the soul,

water and nurture the seed
then the mind blossoms, grows,
and reaches out
to unify with the spirit.
The mind is a tool
when used for its only true purpose
of reconnecting to *Me*.
The material world around man dissolves
and the invisible life
is reclaimed and revealed.

The essence of all that I have created
exists only in divine spirit consciousness.
The mind of man/woman is
designed to find his or her way
back to *Me*.

The question:
is creation a game
that only I can win?
The answer is
there is never
a winner or a loser.

It is just a reflection
of eternity creating
and recreating itself.

This is *My* design to
experience and self-express
all that I have created.

Every face of creation
is *Me*,
animal, mineral, and vegetable.

I have no mind or
need for one
because *I AM*
the creator
of all life
and life's reflections.

When man learns
how to dissolve his mind,
he will clearly see *Me*
in his reflection.
He and I are ONE
in the same.

Cleansing the Soul

This is an act of defiance by man
who thinks he was self-created.
The soul purges and renews itself
through all earthly experiences.
The mind navigates
where the soul needs to purify and purge.

Man's mind when not used properly
acts as a veil, clouding and disguising
the path that leads to purification
and cleansing of the soul.

In the beginning of man's existence,
he had peace and paradise
until he misused his mind
to distort knowledge,
which is only pure and everlasting.

Man's mind separated him
from his soul
and he falsely believed that his soul
had no influence over his mind.
He saw them as separate entities.

Through his misconception and mind ego,
he began to multiply
and destroy his own center of peace
and kicked himself out of paradise.

Once man discovers his power to cleanse his soul
by releasing the hold over himself
that he allowed his mind to command,
the soul goes direct
and restores man
back to his original place in paradise.

Peace

When everything is all right with you and the world,
how do you know you have reached the place of peace?
If you have to ask, you are not there yet!

There are no days or tomorrows.
There is no time for rushing or earthly stresses.
There is respect and conscious living
with and among every living creature I have created.
There is no longing or sorrow for sought after things
or times that have moved on.

The landscape changes constantly
even if you are dwelling in a single room.
The mind is active but no longer questioning anything.
There is no place for judgment
of anything walking the Earth,
working to return to *Me*.

There only exists an unconditional love
and acceptance of what you have been given
to express and experience
for *Me* through *Me*.

All is well above and below.
All is in order and there is no time
waiting for anything.

Everything is in constant motion of evolution.
There is no time.
There is only peaceful joy
filled with fulfillment
of the soul's earthly journey
to return to the ONE.

Living the Life of Extremes

Extremism is the mischief
and improper use of the mind.
Extremism is motivated
by an individual's need
to be recognized by others
and a non-belief
that he or she is not good enough.

I ask why is man or woman
so bent on keeping their mind earth-bound,
struggling with judgments of one another
and seeking to find *Me*?

I AM not hidden
or only visit on special occasions.
I AM forever present,
but I have given man
eternity to find *Me*
and return home.

Extremism is another road
more traveled than not.
Until an individual realizes
the competition with the self

is never-ending when the mind
has become your master
and not the spirit.

Nothing can ever be forced
because it already exists
in its perfect state of being.

The pattern of spiritual awakening
has a definite path and envelopment
that each individual will experience.
No one knows when the enfoldment comes
until he or she
stops being led by their mind
and hears My voice.

What they seek is not without but within.
You cannot force awakening.
It is only I who will let you know the time.

Even My son Jesus does not have
the ultimate power
to awaken mankind.
He is the living symbol and verification
that you too can enter the kingdom.
Only I and I alone can summon you.

Believe not the false prophets to decry
the power they possess to teach mankind
how to become awakened.

There is no meditation, herb, or potion
that will open the soul.

They themselves are seekers.
The prophets I have placed among man
never decry that their teaching
is the only road back to *Me*.
There is no force ever exerted
through diet, dreams, deprivation,
and denial of the material world.
I do not demand or require such.

When the stillness becomes
your companion and only friend,
then and only then has the condition been set
and the path cleared for *Me*
to look deep inside to know if you
are ready to hear and receive *Me*.
Then and only then.

Forbearance

What is there to endure
when a heart's intentions are pure?

Forbearance is not a labor,
but an act of divine strength
to be patient,
to let *My* work on Earth
reach fruition.
Nothing is ever given to man
that cannot be endured
and taught patience
for all things I set into motion.

Forbearance is a time of ripening
for all things
to be made manifest to mankind.

Some have mastered waiting.
Others are still trapped
in their manmade timetables.

NOW you know why eternity exists
to return to *Me*.

Contrition

Since the beginning of the world, man has taken the act of contrition ever so lightly. Mankind has thought how words during confession sufficed to eradicate their behavior. Inside the hollowness of these words uttered for forgiveness leaves room only for repeat performances of their misdeeds. The act of contrition is not a confession, but a purification of one's soul through understanding the purity that exists in *My* name and in *My* name only. *My* existence is only to reflect pure love through mankind. When man strays from this purpose, he is operating outside of his soul. He has totally surrendered to the universal negativity that is operating by man's own design. This is not *My* creation. When an act of contrition is done, the soul is flooded with pure light and love and never repeats the offense for all eternity. The words of man's apologies to one another are often hollow and misplaced because to create an offense, it's not against only one individual, but an offense against *Me* and what *I AM* reflecting to the world. True repentance is to seek forgiveness in the pure light of love through *Me* and *Me* only.

The Process of Doing

Man is conditioned by his own self-direction to perform for satisfaction and/or reward for doing. Man has centered his doing on motivation or inspiration. The process of doing has no rewards or acts that are valued as great or small. The process of doing is the process balance in the universe. Every soul is assigned something to do and carry forward. Man has set up a reward scale and notoriety to report to the world what has been done or is about to be done. The process of doing is the process of refinement. Remember nothing on Earth is new under the sun. Refinement of doing, acts like a strainer that sifts out wheat, separating, it from its chaff. It is the entire kernel of wheat man uses for nourishment. Everything is cloaked until revealed to the soul of man. Lessons would have no reason to be continually taught if man was not making his own rules to redirect himself. To do what is needed, is a process of automatic response without question or validation of outcome. There is great joy in doing anything with pure intention and love. A doer never looks back to see a reflection of an outcome of a deed that is done. There is no righteousness in the act of doing. A man of God knows the source of all goodness comes from *Me* and is not misled by false prophets or false ego. A man of God knows he is being used as the instrument to carry forth the act of doing what I have asked of mankind. Earth Man's intellectual folly has completely obscured the joy of doing. He sees the doing as a job on giving him recognition and material satisfaction. These are thoughts fed by man's ego. When the shield is dropped by the awakening of *My* son the Christ within man, then man will recognize him as the true reason for doing everything from love. Think of counting every drop it took to fill the ocean being counted. How will you ever have an account when I will always send rain to nurture the Earth? There is no counting or keeping track of the process of doing. It is essential to nurture man, as the rain is essential to nurture the Earth.

Guilt and Blame

These are two emotions that impede the path to healing and truth. Man needs to shift the responsibility of each individual's wrong doing onto another and justify the reason for the shift. Guilt is the reflex that happens when man knows the responsibility has been shifted elsewhere. He must confess and acknowledge any and all transgressions man has knowingly committed. There is no such thing as an unconscious act. The act that is committed is a repressed emotion that activates the mind to take action and do the deed. The soul is aware of the games man is playing with his mind, but before the journey begins home, man will confess his sins and transgressions before *Me*.

Spiritual Cleansing

Man, ancient and modern, thinks he has found the key to cleanse one's soul. Cleansing does not work like a carwash where you take your car every week. Cleansing is being bathed in *My* pure divine light. When I bathe you with *My* light, you are cleansed for eternity. Total knowledge and practice of surrender are the prerequisites. When I speak of knowledge, *I AM* not talking about seminary degrees or certifications of long-term practices. *I AM* referencing one's ability to stand totally alone and embrace *Me* without any doubt or fear. You wake up looking to *Me* first before beginning your day's journey. You look to *Me* for counsel and guidance when you feel unsure. You let *Me* fill your day with love and a multitude of blessings. You do these things with joy and acceptance that this is your rightful place with *Me*. When you can wake and walk with *Me* every day of your earth life, you have one foot into eternity by *My* side. Only I can purify your ignorance and arrogance to rule a world that is not yours to rule.

Compensation

Everyone is looking to receive something for good performance or deed. Man has set up this reward system. The under achievers always stand in the shadow of judgment man has created. When I created the world and put man in it, I did not look for compensation for this act. I created the world and put man in it to share and explore the many facets of *My* enduring and eternal love for man and all that I created. The question is if this is so, then why are people not sharing equal in the dividing of the pie? Why? Because I gave man free will to live in paradise and simple rules: love *Me* and only *Me* and love thy neighbor as thyself. The free will of man gives him the opportunity to use the mind creatively and humanly. Selfish motivation of the material things man has created, such as enterprise, money, and luxuries, set him immediately apart from doing things for the common good of man. Through selfishness, man divided and conquered all he had amassed. No different today than when I first created the world. The task remains the same: how to continue to work with *My* creation on the soul level independent of free will and the mind. *I AM* still working on this process of self-expression. There is nothing before *Me* or after *Me*. *I AM* all that is man when he is reflecting pure light and love back to *Me* through his soul expression of pure divine love.

To Secure Your Place Within *Me*

In order to return to *Me* within *Me*
to be reabsorbed by *Me*
you have to have mastered
being a perfect mirror.
You are a mirror
that only reflects to the world
emanating from *Me*.

Your aging mirror reflects
how you have reflected *Me*
to the world.
I have not put sickness upon anything
I have created for the world.

Man has used free will
and selfish enterprises
toward mankind.
The reflection of love is dimmed
by those thought forms.

I know everything about
every creature
and what living man is reflecting
to the world at all times.

If I created man in *My* own image
and blew the breath of life into the being,
I also gave man instruction,
how to live in the world I made for him.

Nothing was ever created
that did not have
simple but specific rules to abide by.
The rules have not been changed by *Me,*
but by man.
To be reabsorbed,
man must journey back
to his beginning of pure love
that created him in the first place.

No one is ever rejected a return.
But the struggle to release man's will
as it is in conflict with *My* will to
only give the world love
is man's conflict.
When he sees pure love
in his soul reflection,
then and only then
is he viewing the world
through the eyes of GOD.

Peace Be Still

Peace is the calm of the rivers
and the oceans at sunset.
Peace is the slumber of a soul
resting from a day
well served and put to bed.
Peace is a walk that is wordless of preaching.
It is a walk of awareness
of everything that exists on Earth
in and out of conflict.
Peace is a seesaw
forever going up and down
and balancing on occasion.
Peace is work done on the inside of man
and manifests in his deeds toward all humanity.
Peace has no measure.

Diligence

Diligence is not synonymous with patience. To be diligent in all that one does is to bear the fruits of the effort. The concept of time cheats man to create as close to perfection as possible. There is always some unforeseen deadline man sets up before he does anything. There is this secret internal self-judgment committee that man feels is waiting to pass judgment on his creations. The highest form of creation is when you are in communion with *Me* and allow *Me* the freedom to express myself through you. I can open the portal of this expression at any given opportunity when I know you have put your busy mind to rest with all the things you are thinking creates everything. To be diligent in all you do is to honor and know the source of all creation. I have no clock or deadline to bring anything into existence. Creating is as natural as breathing when not constricted by man's own thoughts and his need to sever the time stressors he has created.

Absolution

〜⌒〜

This is the process of being rooted and confirmed in *My* existence. No matter what the distraction, you are not deterred from your belief in *Me*. When one is absolute, he/she has reached an unshakeable stance and has digested all the eternal world has to offer. They have moved into the invisible realm that does not offer possibilities created by man's mind, but the soul bears witness to the world from which it came. Can man live a dual existence between both worlds? Absolutely is the answer. It is man's unnerving, unshakeable faith and knowledge that *I AM*, which I gave to the prophets. They were necessary because man was so dense and blocked by relating to the material world and false gods. Through spiritual evolution and spiritual experimentation, man was able to look into the invisible world without fear of loss of his material world. As man became more absolute in his spiritual experiences after the resurrection of *My* son, then the belief systems began to evolve. Man has moved but is still locked by fear. World oppression and religious division and persecution are evidence of this. Eternity is necessary. Eternity is like a spiritual workspace where you get the opportunity to become absolute in the belief of *Me* and all I have created to experience and express *My* love to the world I and I alone created.

Nullification of *My* Existence

To nullify *My* existence is ego arrogance reinforced by the negative thoughts man surrounds himself with. There are no questions in the universe. It is because it always was.

Man's mind has made him inflexible to believe in anything he cannot manipulate or make manifest in the material realm. Everything man thinks he controls is in his mind. The soul doesn't ever operate on the level of control, power, or constant obstacles to test truth. The soul knows all and is constantly looking at the individual's reasoning capabilities to navigate while on Earth. Man, since the beginning, has felt he knows more and better than I do how the world is run or should be run. It is the free will, which I gave man to reason as a navigational tool that is misused and out of alignment with *Me*. Lessons learned and lessons taught are the refinement and tuning tools used to bring man back to inner focus on the *I AM*.

If man still remains confounded about what came first, the chicken or egg, how does he possibly think he created himself? His ego has created manmade sciences that he thinks he can create and clone life of *My* creatures and of him. Every experiment is flawed. If man was trying to create life out of love, peace, and abundance for all to share, then maybe he would have *My* blessing and sanction with these sciences, but the arrogant ego says I do not exist and man has free reign of *My* world and universe. He will have eternity to find the road that leads back to *Me* and on only *Me*.

Tranquility

This is a state of balance in the mind, body, and spirit. The alignment of the soul is in direct accord with everything and everyone in the universe. The soul always seeks this state. If the soul is deprived of this state of being, the mind becomes agitated, so much so that turmoil is ever present in one's life. The tranquil state allows man to breathe on his own with engaging any thought process. Tranquility is not always obtained by prayer and meditations. Sometimes it is achieved by shutting down the mind, which is always working. This shift in consciousness can take place anywhere and at any time. It's like a powerful engine of a train that suddenly looses energy to move at full speed and has shut down to just chugging along. The train is still powerful in form, but the internal mechanisms have been altered. Tranquility is *My* way of giving man a rest and a look inside the realm from which he was created. It is a surprise for many when it happens to them and it is a place to be embraced by others who have been working on lessening the constant engagement of their mind. Tranquility is one of the many gifts man can receive with *My* blessing.

Kindreds - Truth & Faith

Trust and Faith are constantly being tested by their nemesis Doubt. If Doubt gets even a pinky toe into the door of Trust and Faith, it can keep the door ajar. When a spirit is recycled through to keep manifesting *My* will in creation, so much of the past Fear and Doubt have been removed from the memory of past experiences. However, the important lesson that must be taught on Earth to share and teach others is dormant until an experience awakens the past memory. This process is in place for every soul until their return to *Me* and a completion of the *I AM* ONE is fully manifested. Trust and Faith are quiet acts. They are acts that make manifest every time the soul awakens one's body. Beware of those preaching how to master Trust and Faith. If the individual has become a master, it will shine like a lighthouse beacon on a dark ocean. The individual's presence is calming and soothing to the soul, like a healing balm. These souls are not boastful or asking for material wealth to lead their fellow man's footstep to the path of *My* kingdom. Trust and Faith are conditions of the inner world, not the outer world. The kindness holds up and supports one another; the presence of fear of the unknown invisible world is what makes man's travels so sluggish.

Somewhere along the path, the mind planted a seed of fear and the roots took hold and laced themselves into the reasoning chamber of the mind and slowed down man's ability to use discernment. Think of discernment as a seesaw. It fluctuates up and down by the amount of pressure applied. When the pressure is not present and both sides have equal amounts, the perfect balance of the seesaw happens. Man is very much like the seesaw because of the amount of pressure he takes into his life. His only gauge to tell him how he is reacting to pressure of outside forces is to engage Trust and Faith into his life. The material world is one of the most elusive things I have created for man to navigate his return to *Me*. If man believes he has passed the test because of his material gains, he has already failed. But if his seesaw is balanced by sharing of his wisdom and kindness, he has bestowed on his fellowman, and then he has learned the meaning of the kindred Trust and Faith and put them into action in the universe.

Despondency

When a soul is despondent, it is a sign they are disconnected from *Me*. The individual has allowed the effects of negative groups' soul expression to seep into their being. Think of driving to an unknown place and not following directions that were given or misinterpreting a map you cannot read. All directions to peace, love, fellowship are in plain view. But man is more preoccupied with the complex tangled thought that he thinks defines intellect. Some of *My* best messengers I have sent to Earth to awaken man's slumber are not of man's intellectual institutionalized training. Why? Because life is experienced in the world being exposed to everyday living and practicing simple tasks and simple loving deeds. Man's mind has set up great institutions to himself, not to *Me*. When asked, "Do you know *Me*?" the answer is often *I AM* relegated to religious studies or seminaries exclusively. The answer is never, "Yes, I know him. He is everywhere and in everything." This thought is the most disappointing to man and adds to the despondency of what man has created in the world and thinks he controls. Therefore, joyousness is not in abundance in the existence of man until he learns *I AM* everything and everyone.

Peace in All Things

Peace is balance maintained and restored in all things. *Same as above; same as below.* The universe is an orbiting of energy fed by *My* power to maintain balance. All planets have their unique purpose in the universe. Some provide light, sound, climate controls, and the workplace for *My* creations. Man introduced chaos on the planet Earth. His mind is the constant nemesis to peace on his planet. His mind has been fed so much chaos that man believes this is the natural order of his earth life. Man cannot find peace until he works on his self-created chaos. All on Earth are affected. I should say infected. But the cure is in front of man's very eyes, but it is not the eyes of seeing that is required to bring peace to Earth. It is the inner soulic eye that must be discovered and explored to initiate peace. As the universe continues, so does man in his quest to find peace.

Trust and Know that I am the Beginning Without End

Everyone's walk with *Me* is a personal walk. The lessons for man are the same for all, but the road they choose is chosen by their endowed free will. Man's mind, when not in accordance with the recognition of *My* existence, needs and demands proof of everything to validate and document. This is where he moved since the day when I flooded the earth with prophets to guide and awaken him. Technologies have placed Man into an outer world to keep the mind constantly stimulated. Even when man is not technologically engaged, his mind is thirsty for reengagement between the lulls. Man's mind makes him think he is recreating in heaven and on Earth. The entertaining point is that man is running in circles like a dog chasing his tail, discovering what already is or has never ceased to be.

Knowledge follows wisdom. But man is on a tread-mill to misuse knowledge, which he has rediscovered, to mistreat that planet he lives on and to mistreat his brothers and sisters who share the planet. This is not a display of knowledge becoming wisdom. The cycle of life begins and continues through *Me*. Think of the process as refining. *I AM* working the process of man to become pure love. This is the total countenance of *My* expression throughout the universe. The enlightened soul does not struggle with who *I AM* and where I came from and how I exist. The enlightened soul knows he or she is *Me* inside. They are looking at *My* creation through their eyes as I continually hone and refine the process of creation and all the life forms that live and travel *My* universe. Trust and know the end of physical life is just a chapter closed and another one beginning in the book of eternal life.

Past and Future Comfort

The past and the future are not your favorite comforters you reach to cuddle with. The past and the future are non-existent. You only have the NOW to work with your soul development. The memories you have stored are memories stored by the mind like a mental photograph. This mental reference library is necessary to balance against how much your soul is progressing in the NOW. How many times have you repeated a lesson until it is learned? How many times has the lesson appeared to be disguised? How many times have you used your spiritual eye and not your physical eye to discern the situation? How many times have you used your spiritual ear as opposed to your inner ear to really listen at the depth necessary before the soul will render a decision to move forward? The soul is decisive. The mind is the mechanism that stores and turns information over and over for review of the mind to make sure all details are captured. Eternity is always NOW. When you pray for forgiveness, does it apply to the deed that has already happened? The prayer you are sending to *Me* is always in the NOW because the feeling of needing to be forgiven is their NOW. One can never divorce him or herself from the NOW because the past and the future do not exist. The mind will store the best memories and the not-so-good memories as landmarks for spiritual growth. If you are tied to either memory, past or future, you have not moved into the NOW. How many times have you made plans and when you were ready to act on it, the circumstances have totally changed and require a different response in the NOW? *I AM* not saying that planning is a negative activity. What *I AM* saying is trying to have control over the events of the NOW is an impossibility.

Think of it this way. Planning is self-validation for *Me* to gauge the progress in all he or she does in their earth life. The ego wants recognition and appreciation for deeds. The mind drives the ego, so the stronger the ego, the greater the drive. The egoless worker is always working in the NOW and doesn't need to take stock of his or her achievements because the doing is more important than recognition and praise. The doing acts like air supply to the enlightened. They can never get enough of breathing in the sweet cleansing air that blows through the spirit to empty out so he or she can receive more doing. They pray to *Me* to be an empty vessel for *Me* to fill in the NOW. They have come to the soul enlightenment that ALL IS ONE and the work serves only one purpose, the purpose of the ONE. *I AM* You, You are *Me*, We are Us, and Us are Them forever in eternity.

Opportunity

The opportunity is always and forever NOW. Because time is nonexistent, all action taken by any individual is never action that is passive. What do I mean by non-passive action? Every thought man promotes is action. The fact that until man recognizes the mind for what it is and engages in his spiritual activities on Earth, his actions are scattered and misdirected. The individuals on the road to spiritual enlightenment hear less and less mind chatter as they move along the path. They invite more and more tranquility into their lives when they become aware of *My* presence within them. The opportunity is ever present for man to choose the path of good deeds and good will on Earth. However, man's mind is trained in distraction as a form of personal entertainment for the mind. The mind, when not properly directed is always seeking the opportunity to test man's existence. The soul knows there is eternity in *Me* and does not move away or struggle for the unification of the ONE. The soul knows man is given every opportunity in the NOW to seek the opportunity to be awakened to the true self, *Me,* living forever within man.

Profundity

Man is always seeing through his mind everything in existence that has appeared in some profound way. Man cannot or will not, but eventually will come to full consciousness that he has created nothing. He is not a magician who reaches into the hat and pulls out a rabbit. That is the oldest trick in the magician's handbook. Man has created the illusion of reality by tricking his mind to believe all he has created is real. Everything man has used on Earth has been borrowed from the ethers and materially manifested and vaporized when the illusion is no longer needed. The archeologists study the past ruins and artifacts to where man came from and they tell him why man is where he is today. It sounds simple, but the equation is man + mind + matter = illusion. Man can manifest from his mind what he wants his reality to be. Thus, when man's intentions to create are not filled with love for humanity and the blessed planet, which I have given him, then man manifests and makes his monstrosities in the world that is of no service to mankind at all, but only becomes self-serving. He creates all types of profound institutions, events, and wealth as a monument to his ability as a thinker and doer.

The wise man's profundity is sought after by living a simple life, doing simple deeds, and moving around the earth with respect and reverence for the life the planet sustains. Notoriety exceeds profundity. Everything must have some kind of shock value in order for man to con-firm and fall in line to confirm his existence of him in the world. It has become an extremely important shift of consciousness away from the material world and move in the direction of feeding Earth's inhabitants' soul food. An action of righteousness is what is needed for the meal of the day. Man has destroyed so many things and he cannot repair them. Neither is he trying to repair the massive holes he has torn in universal consciousness with his love and quest for material wealth. Today, man is not worshiping the golden calf; he has replaced the calf with the microchip. Man has moved himself into the world of technology, which he says only deals with logic. The logic man is serving to the world is not only destructive and disruptive, but has proven time and time again to be a repeat of how he has learned to live on his planet. The desire to be fed by profundity complicates man's existence. It does not simplify his existence, and deters and (at times) stagnates movement that returns him. This is only one of the reasons I have given man eternity to work on his return home.

The Fraudulent Spirit

What is this you are questioning? How can a spirit be fraudulent if a human has only one soul? Isn't the spirit the part that returns to *Me* when it is awakened, enlightened, and has done the work I required on Earth? How can the soul perpetrate a fraudulent appearance? All of these are natural questions to be pursuant of the answer. How this exists in the world and continues to make manifest is when the mind has been co-opted by thought forms that are not directed for the good of the whole. Remember, if *I AM* You and You are *Me,* then We are Us and Us are Them. The thought forms projected by man conjure up to do harm, manifest greed, and be unkind to the planet. They are not deeds that emanate from *Me* the One. *My* soul expression is love pure and simple. There is no equation or complex formula to decipher. Straight at you, Love + Love = Love. However, the equations that man concocts on the Earth are not of this formula and therefore have created, as you will think of these creations, spiritual robots, told when to do and how to do and who to do it to.

This group soul thought form keeps man's vibration grounded on the dense astrophysical plane, leaving little space for ascension. Look at it as a massive traffic jam, only instead of anything physical you see, it is a snare of congested thoughts tangled on Earth. How does one extricate him/herself from the snare you ask? It starts with an inventory of wants vs. desires vs. needs. Question your motivation and commitment to the material world. Can you assess the value of fellowship and brother/sisterhood beyond judgments of material worth? Have you been able to stop the never-ending stream of thoughts streaming in one direction of the material path? What are the lessons learned and taught from each and every disappointment or heartache? Question yourself. Are you a leader or a follower or both in one? This is just the scratch on the surface of the dialogue necessary to free the soul from the mental traffic-jam man created. Who is in the driver's seat at all times? Who has orchestrated the path to lead the way to return to the One? Is it you or is it *Me*? Are you a part of *Me*, or do you belong to the mind I created? Have you stood and watched your soul watching your behaviors? Are you a believer in good and evil, right vs. wrong, past vs. future, beginning vs. end, value vs. invaluable? These are belief systems and evaluations man has created to orchestrate and navigate his earth walk. These are the judgments man believes keeps him going, makes him/her a man/woman of God. These thoughts are the imbalanced thoughts of the fraudulent soul broadcasting its existence in the world. The search for the pure loving living spirit dwells deep within like an undiscovered spring that will quench the soul for all eternity. How many are ready or desire to make the climb inside to descend to the spring? Many get glimpses of this place, but they look away because they feel all earthly treasures they have amassed will vanish and they are no longer relevant in the eyes of the fellowman/woman.

The self-expressed soul is not the unification of *My* love, but the dividing line like the one on the highways stating *stay in your lane*. The soul has no restriction. It has the open road to travel. No map to follow. The journey is guided by listening internally and the patience to hear *My* voice speaking to you. When man learns to do this, then he is prepared to be fully endowed to express *My* love to the world. The soul's life is no longer a jigsaw puzzle. It becomes seamless.

The Beauty of Creation

Beauty is just that—beautiful. Not because it is *My* creation, but because beauty is the signification of harmony when all come together for the One. *Me*, I, You, Them, Us, We is reflected in a raindrop, sunset, budding leaf, a newborn birthing, a perfect cloud, a sound of aum/om vibrating and harmonizing the universe. This is the beauty of creation. It is not deposited in vaults at banks. It has a never-ending supply that constantly blends and fills the canvas of a soul's Earth journey. Tear up any piece of concrete constructed on Earth and as you strip away the layers, you will find the soil of Mother Earth moist and full like a woman's breast designed to feed her young. Stargazers can propel their vision into space and can never count the never-ending galaxy of stars. Day into night, night into day, revolving endlessly, tirelessly moving in or suspended in a universal space holding harmony and beauty.

Man thinks this beauty is like a paint-by-numbers game. Select the color and put it there. The beauty I've made for man is layered on Earth and in the galaxies. Man's destructiveness has stripped away areas of earthly beauty. Only I can or will determine if it should be replaced. Earthquakes, tsunamis, severe storms are warnings to man to live lovingly and peacefully on *My* Earth. Nothing that ever happens on Earth or in heaven is an unplanned occurrence. Man is busy calculating this event and that event, but is always in the element of surprise by his predictions. If man read the events of the Old Testament, he would see the error of his earthly ways. These stories are not myths. The writers have embellished some here and there to keep the reader's interest, but the events for those who recorded them are true. And after all of that, time and time again I restored man to live in a place of beauty.

When you see the beauty of nature destroyed, it is not *My* doing. I make adjustments to the population from time to time, but do not use nature as a weapon to eradicated beauty. Man is solely responsible for that. He calls it progress to run people off the land to drill for oil, to build housing for specific groups of people, decides to be the superman who has poisoned rivers and streams and has poisoned the air with factories. Man calls this progress to advance mankind. The simple thing in the earthly experience is the free man has decided to clog the flow and replace it with unequal distribution to all. It is an ageless and timeless experience, the awakening evolution of the soul. Beauty will exist as a reminder that *I AM* always here. *I AM* forever watching, working, waiting for man's acknowledgement that his is part of the ONE and not an individual entity.

The Dalliance of Man

You can detain your evolution by the act of standing still. The commercials depict fast-paced action, darting from one scene to another. Man is much like the commercials he creates. Man is restless, always seeking to discover what is already in place. This rushing action is the same as standing still. Not much is achieved by the shuffling of random thoughts man gleans from his discoveries. The man/woman who sits in meditation with *Me* is the man/woman on the rise. The man/woman who is moving his/her position closer and closer to doing world good deeds are the ones who are able to see the world as it really is and the conflicts man has created for himself. The sitting man/woman is in motion. The sitting man/woman has released his mind of earthly thoughts. This man/woman knows not the experience of dalliance. In man's mind, there is always tomorrow to complete what he/she has started. They believe in the promise of a never-ending tomorrow. This thought process causes the soul to move in a stop-start pattern. This thinking interferes with the natural flow already preset for man's evolutionary process to return to the One.

Thoughts of tomorrow leads to the introduction of flow that man calls procrastination. He/she knows and feels the natural flow of momentum moving forward but allows negative thoughts to enter that create an interruption in the flow. When they start to restart their reengagement after their period of procrastination, there appears to be a feeling of loss, loss of time, loss of completion. There is a feeling of being behind and an anxiety to play hurry up and catch up. Every execution of anything acted upon always happens in the NOW. Even periods of procrastination introduced by the mind becomes the NOW when the individual begins to re-engage in their life. Procrastination is a pit stop for self-imposed fatigue by over-thinking everything and being a prisoner of time.

Intolerance

Intolerance is an expression of passive judgment on an individual, place, or thing. Everything and every human have the right to exist, *My* decree. No one can stand in judgment of anyone or anything. The act of intolerance is an act of judgment against *Me*. You are judging *Me* to be flawed and imperfect. All of you "do right, never do wrong" humans who prove to follow *My* words in the Bible are intolerant of others who worship *Me* and pray to *Me* in a different tongue or are reading another text. What makes you think I have different lessons and teachings for them than I have you? You call yourselves the followers of God, spreading *My* word, yet you are intolerant of all others who do not follow your doctrine. *My* doctrine says love thy neighbor as thyself and put no other God before *Me*. Two simple requests, but these requests have made man fearful and intolerant to live in harmony. What would make humans think I have preferential treatment for humans in one geographical location over another? What would make humans think their cluster of humans are the Chosen Ones over another cluster of humans? Man put the mandate on Earth than men are not created equal. Loving thy neighbor as thyself has become a metaphor to travel the Earth to preach false doctrines, plunder, and subject brothers and sisters to poverty and fear. In the world that I created for man, there is no reason whatsoever for humans to be hungry and without shelter. But these conditions exist because of intolerance and lack of compassion to love they neighbor as thyself. Intolerance is a lack of God knowledge in one's soul. Even if the smallest flicker arises in a being, there is work to be done on your soul. When you profess to love *Me* and follow *My* teachings, explore your area of intolerance and see where you stand. In order to banish intolerance, man must first make his/her peace with the material world and his/her belief in a lack of anything on the Earth. Man has created the lack of what man needs to exist on Earth. Man needs to exist on Earth. Man can return to the garden but he cannot and will not be allowed to enter as long as he is partnered with intolerance and greed.

My Word and *My* Will

Everything I gave to man in promise is through *My* will. I have asked man to follow *My* word and *My* will with all promises fulfilled. *I AM* true to *My* world because the word is *My* creation. I have given man no less than I would give myself. All on Earth is a self-expression of *Me* to be actualized through man. All that is an expression of love and abundance is through *My* will. Man wants to place the blame on someone or something when he/she has disobeyed *My* word. There is always some excuse because the world man lives in is not perfect. It is always some outside forces changing the course man wants to pursue. If man had truly learned how to navigate on Earth and allow his/her true spirit to chart and navigate the journey on Earth, then nothing would trouble the water, the sky, and the Earth, which is where he/she resides. *I AM* speaking in terms of him/her because they are One in a united soul. Man has yet to realize that woman is half his whole self. She is part of his whole. His decisions without her included are lopsided. Both of them paid their price in their abuse of paradise. They are not cursed or banished from Eden. Their acts on the Earth determine if they will find their way back. *I AM* both male and female in *My* expression to the world. I cannot be split into one or the other. To honor the parts that are male and female is to honor the whole of *Me*.

Birth is not the process of cloning, which Earth scientists experiment with to create life. Birth is the process of refinement of the soul to keep entering until the process of pure love is expressed in the world. It is *My* will that mandates this process to be necessary for soul expression. It is *My* world and *My* will that determines how man is progressing on Earth. It is *My* will that life's every lesson is taught and charted on the course I have set for the soul. The soul is guided by *My* will to follow the path. Man has allowed the act of disobedience to follow the path laden with obstacles produced by man's mind and ego. These detours are self-made and deter the return to the One. It is *My* will guided by *My* words, which leads to the liberation and unification of the soul's return to *Me*, unite to the One. *My* world and *My* will decree this process. This is the process of the return to the kingdom of *My* heavenly home.

The Gathering of Souls

When man allows his mind to run away with ill intentions toward the Earth and his fellow man, I bring together a community of souls to restore some order in man's self-made chaos. These souls gather together at various places on the Earth. Some leave in great numbers, by floods, earthquakes or what man calls natural disasters. False prophets prophesize the end of the world is coming or is about to come when they witness these events. The souls taken are doing *My* work to teach man how sacred life is, and it can be easily transformed. The events are a gathering in two forms. The gathering of souls who are departing to teach the lessons, and the souls left behind to transform the lives others for the better.

Wars are manmade events. Man decides whom he wants to invade in a display of power, greed, and self-hatred. War is not *My* creation. War is brought about by free will. War ends when man decides there is nothing to gain. There are also gatherings of souls who are lookers balancing love and healing on Earth. These souls have become instruments of healing at the highest level to receive the blessings to be bestowed on humans who have lost their way on the path and will be restored. There are other gathered souls who work in tandem to support these light workers. A good shepherd never leaves his flock unattended. A good shepherd finds all strays and potential runaways and returns them to the flock. Man has a physical life span on Earth to figure out what type of shepherd he/she wants to be in *My* flock. Blessed are the Lambs of God who turn to *Me* and only *Me* to lead them.

The Light Under the Rock

"Well I run to the rock to hide your face. The rock cried out "No hiding place. There's down here." Music has a transformational healing quality. Each note executed and transformed into sound resonates to millions upon millions and countless of humans who are open to receive it. The light under the rock means man should not listen to anyone directing them and assuring them they will wake into the light. The awakening to light consciousness is *My* business. Words, directions and suggestions are bountiful on Earth, but until man can hear *Me* and feel *Me* touching their soul within, they have been looking for the light under the rock. Man knows there is some force out there unknown to his mind's perception. His unwillingness to accept this as fact is a delayed response constantly being triggered by the brain. Don't accept this unknown, this which you cannot touch, taste, feel, or manipulate. Look under the rock. Maybe the secret is there as man digs in the Earth for buried treasure and his past. This is backward thinking. Imagine how man would travel the Earth if his feet were placed behind him to walk and his head and eyes remain at the front of the skull. He would start walking backward while looking forward. What a confused state of looking at the scenery of life moving away from you rather than coming at you.

The past and the present have merged into a confused vision. Everything on Earth is always present and always NOW. Has learning how the humans on Earth or in another dimension of man's time stopped man's love for war, hatred, destruction of the planet, producing false prophets and witnesses? Has all this historical digging enabled man to use what he has learned to replicate the power of love and eradicate the poison of hate on this planet? The historians talk about the blood sacrifices used in rituals and the sacrificing of humans to their gods. What has changed with the sacrifices made to scientific experiments throughout the course of man to worship the god of science, which man created? Nothing is new on Earth. Man can never be the judge of what he negatively created. I and I alone know what man is capable of. I and I alone determine when his experimental time on Earth is done. When man has learned to personify and reflect pure love toward creation, then and only then is he shown the light within him and is absorbed by *Me*.

Mind of Mind

The mind is like a tractor plowing the ground before planting. The farmer can be seen as the soul who sits upon the tractor, directing its motion through row by perfect row of plowing. If the tractor is left unattended with the engine still running in motion, the tractor can and will run amuck and destroy the rows that have been perfectly plowed by the soul driver. Everything is on a collision course on the planet when the soul is not leading the mind. Man releasing himself through his mind is like taking your hands off the wheel of a moving car. Anything can happen upon impact. A disconnect is created by man's mind and free will.

What is Free Will?

Free will is the space within the soul to make choices of movement in their life walk. The mind is also connected to this free will. The free will makes the choice of good for the whole and for the self as it relates to itself, as an individual before it realizes throughout its earth journey is part of the One. Free will is a navigational tool man can use to move freely on Earth. It is how this free will works in tandem with the mind to do goodness on Earth that is the challenge. When man discovers the soul within is a part of the One, his universe becomes a beautiful place that vibrates and transmits love to all living beings. It is resurrecting of soul consciousness to ascend to the One that is the ultimate goal. All is in balance, peace, harmony and eternal love. No one knows their departure from the Earth. No one needs to know. All that is necessary to know is that the work of his/her soul discovery is the reward of their earth journey.

Seriousness of One's Faith

Your earth walk is your reflecting pool as you walk and do deeds to others on this Earth. It is all reflected back to *Me*. Nothing can ever be hidden or unnoticed. *I AM* the constant to all life. If I were not, it would be like giving a blind man a sports car and turning him loose to drive on the freeway. The freeway of one's earth life is well planned and well measured. Because the work is measured that needs to be done, suicide is not an option. You cannot make your own plan of exit. If you do, you will find yourself back in a physical body and back on Earth reworking your divine plan. I can forgive all things man does with his devotion to his mind as his god. The mind is necessary to navigate on the earth plane, but it is not essential when the body has been transcended.

There is so much exploration of other planets and the universe in search of life forms. Man on Earth was not created to live in other parts of the universe. Man is the least developed in spiritual awareness and has many levels of ascension before he is ready for other realms. What is faith to man but the belief to follow blindly into the acceptance of an invisible form? The sacredness of faith is to learn to surrender to all that exists and to surrender to the entire unknown. Man is constantly being shown his free will as a slide show of his life on Earth. Man has decided what is the point to having a brilliant mind if somebody or someone is in control of it? The ultimate test to man is to know that his questions will never be answered because they are useless and pointless.

All I require is obedience, kindness, and love to continue to maintain and self-express and create in the universe. Once man comes to the realization there is not a he operating as a separate entity, then peace, love, joy, and unity will exist on Earth. Man will never know everything. Why? Because it is an exercise of man's mind. The faith in *My existence and Me* is all that matters. Why? Because, All is only One.

One source, One soul,
One Center, One core,
One seed from where man sprouted.

The Power of Enlightenment

The use of power I reference here is the power transformation of the soul to express *My* will, *My* work, and *My* love throughout the universe. This transformation of consciousness links to the One of All. The soul becomes weightless and timeless in its return home to *Me*. No confusion exists in the mind of man because man has found the path out of duality thinking. Man has transcended time, space, days, weeks, and years as his fellow man relates to manmade concepts. The power is that path of resistance where no questions are proposed. If any ripple of doubt of any kind presents itself, the enlightened one knows the counsel he/she seeks lies within. The answer is always there. The enlightened being in human form cannot escape the humanness of their exact existence, but their seeking has come to an end once they come to the realization *I AM* him/her operating from within.

I AM the genie in the physical bottle. The power lies with knowing this and completing the acts necessary for them to push on the earth plane to assist in the enlightenment of others. This is the purpose of the enlightened soul that has found the connection to the One. Peace through grace is their earth walk. No worries or regrets fill their hearts, minds or souls. They are in complete recognition of their service to mankind. There is no notoriety, no popularity for these souls. If it occurs, it is because I have decreed a spirit to push. It is necessary and everything is accelerated by these works to affect the masses. These souls are like gigantic tidal waves coming ashore to consume and pull man by spiritually awakening the unrest. Some of these individuals are writers, teachers, and lecturers and so on and so on. But it is the unknown, quiet spiritual workers working in the small towns, fortresses, and dark centers of the Earth where man has isolated and barricaded himself in his manmade fortress of power. These enlightened souls do the chopping on the block, bit by bit, until it is a speck of sand. These are the ones who effect the execution of change and it is noted. Blessed are those without notoriety or fame. These are truly *My* Earth angels.

Charity

What is the gift of giving? In man's world, it is measured by material things. The more you give, the more you are looked up to with respect. You are considered a kind hearted individual. Charity in the world man lives in should not exist. Why? Because man has manipulated Earth's resources and has dammed up water supplies and destroyed the resources that feed and supply man's needs on Earth. Man's mind has made him a wayward soul. Taking care of your neighbor, brother, sister, relative, strangers are not negotiated as charity. It is the godly thing to take care of one another. However, if man is the creator of this distribution of wealth to all people, then what good is his charity?

The Earth and hemisphere will erupt to begin again in various parts. The lesson for man because of the choices he makes has made these occurrences necessary to restore man to his common denominator, the beginning of starting a new earth life. The scientists are busy calculating and busying their mind and the minds of men with predictions. Yet they do not use what I have given them to question why these events take place. Scientists will tell you I do not exist. There is no such power that dictates the cause of action through the universe, and on Earth. Yet they are drawn to the mystery of the earth, moon, sky, water, and land. Deep within, they are driven by the mind drug to know the unknown. This is a knowing they will never know. It is not for their knowing because they defy any belief in *Me*. Eternity is so necessary for these souls.

The charity of spirit, however, is an emptying out of all you have experienced on this Earth in your earth life and sharing and uplifting minds and teaching others. These activities should be a constant throughout the Earth by its entire people. All questions man has about his earth life existence need to be examined. Their lives need to be put under the great microscope of life to be looked at. Charity is not a gift, but an indebted act that makes people feel less than those who are giving. Charity is the illusion of caring. How can you give what is every man/woman's right to live on *My* Earth? Who gives you the authority to dam rivers, create toxic waste to feed the Earth, control where food is grown, pay farmers not to grow food, and produce genetically engineered foods that have no life? Who has given man the authority to say what humanity needs? Humanity is not man's creation. The expression of man's charity is useless and pointless until he realizes he is the cause for charity to exist in the first place. When the cover is thrown back off charity, it is revealed that what exists is poverty of man's soul.

The Key to Unlocking
the Mind

∽◯

The key is to not let your thoughts be your reality. They become roadblocks to living in the NOW. Every thought that passes through the mind is a temporary register of what is experienced in the NOW. The memories recalled from the past as man identifies them are still thoughts of the NOW. Thoughts of the so-called future cannot be experienced unless experienced in the NOW. Man stores memories that are painful to his existence. He lets these thoughts live within his being. He feeds and nurtures them every time he brings them forward and then tucks them away. The point of recognizing the NOW is that all healing of these painful thoughts can be healed. Man speaks of forgiveness as the key. Forgiveness is only a fraction of the work to heal. Man must separate from the consciousness of the past and future in order to be healed. Those thoughts are events, but they are not happening in the NOW until you bring them forward from where you have neatly stored them.

A divorce is necessary to heal the sadness and pain of living in the past and the future. You must execute the divorce and the healing is done by *Me*. What removes them is to realize the thoughts have no power in your life. The thoughts do not define what you are and what you came here to do. They are not aware that all they are doing in this world is a reflection of the One. Some souls are more advanced than others. The advanced souls are busy lifting up consciousness of the whole. These souls are clustered together by responsibilities given to them by *Me* and reflect to the world. This process is necessary to continue to do *My* work that reflects to the world through the group. All is One, working as One to eventually unite to the One. They are all navigating the same waters. Each one supports the other to reach God consciousness. Some become enlightened together and begin their walk. Others are still struggling, but will take the walk to consciousness through eternity. Weep not and be sad not of the past and the future because they do not exist. Everything that needs changing and healing can only happen in the NOW, by *Me* and for the NOW.

The Glorious State of Being

Just as is, just as was, just as it is has always been and will forever remain. This state of consciousness is the fully enlightened stage of the soul without form. No more work needs to be done for these ones. No rules have been disobeyed or broken. The soul's earth life has been saturated with nothing but love and forgiveness. His/her work has been done on Earth as it has been in heaven. They have walked in both worlds totally at peace and in harmony with all creation. Blessed are those who did not let the mind present resistance to the work I requested them to reflect to the world. Many of those souls were detached from humanity as a whole, but were still able to bring love, joy, beauty, and peace to the world. Many did their work without notoriety or recognition of any sort. These souls are the foundation of creation. These souls know the value of each contribution to the whole of human existence on Earth. These ones never refer to themselves as *I* or *Me*. These souls embrace all as brothers and sisters. The greatness of these individuals goes unnoticed by the average human on Earth. Why? Because they are busy living in duality of past and future and try to balance their beliefs in good and evil. These are their creations of earthly consumption. These ones that know these are places created by the mind are busy maintaining balance to leave openings in the world for consciousness to begin to evolve. They are committed to eternity to maintain this balance. Blessed are these workers. They are *My* expression that everything has balance in the universe. It is essential to express *My* love to all in *My* creation.

Commitment

Commitment is more than saying to *Me*, yes, Father/Mother/God, I'll do it. To live a life of commitment to *Me* begins with your everyday walk. *I AM* never put on hold for you to perform your earthly mundane tasks. You say *I AM* important, but you allow your mind to talk you adrift and get back to *Me* at your will. This is not commitment. This is distraction by the material world and the humans you decide to serve.

Every being I created has the same journey to return home to *Me*. No human has the power to save another being. It is *My* lessons and will be done on Earth as it is in heaven. It is a struggle for some to break away from human bonds. If you actually believe that *I AM* everyone and everything on Earth and in the universe, than you will realize, *I AM* your best friend. Because *I AM* You, You are *Me*, We are Us and Us are Them. One spirit, one soul, one flesh made manifest to do *My* work of love expressed through the universe through mankind. Man was never made to replace anything on Earth. Man was created by *Me* to experience all things and experience all things through *My* self-expression of love.

Man is *My* mirror, looking glass reflecting back to *Me*, what *I AM* expressing throughout the universe. Commitment is the ability to completely empty yourself of fear, doubt, distrust, manipulation–the need of human companionship is not an expression of pure–love, and the ability to hear *My* voice above others echoing in the universe. Words expressing that you love *Me*, that you desire to follow *My* command, are words that must be called into action at *My* command. There is no rest for the committed. They have more than enough food to fill the spirit. They have on blinders to the distractions and detractors of the world. They hear all but only listen for *My* voice to call them into action. They are the ones touched by *Me* to do *My* work without thought of compensation or reward. Don't get confused by how you are operating on the earth plane. Everything is temporary and constantly dissolving and evolving, one soul experience collapsed into another. The world is full of music, art, healers, and farmers and as many expressions I desire to keep love reflected on the Earth.

There is never a makeover or a starting point. There is only dissolution and rebirth. A committed soul knows no fear of human death. A committed soul never asks to leave the Earth because her/she is tired of what surrounds them. A committed soul has mastered living in worlds, the dense physical and the invisible life. The committed soul can always see through the veil man has surrounded himself with to hide from truth. The committed soul makes no judgments, but moves when called to do the work of *My* kingdom. Know the work of a committed soul is more than a whim, and slip of the lip, wishful thinking. They are the ones that keep creation in balance by *My* will.

Clearance –The Right
to Passage

Ordination to carry *My* work out to the world is given by *Me* only. No ordination is ever imposed on the self. You cannot self-appoint to do this work. The work of an ordinate soul selected by *Me* reaches thousands upon thousands on Earth to stop their path and follow a new way. It is the way of the Christ. Man's free will intertwined with the material world takes many twists and turns. Man is always testing his free will against *Me*. It is a game he never wins. Nevertheless he enjoys engaging in testing the brain he has been given. But the wise man knows the brain is only a tool for the soul to navigate the earth plane.

Clearance is given when man has learned the balance necessary to be in both worlds. Man is a never-ending experience of love. When he goes astray, he is recalled to begin again. Man is forgiven anything he has done on Earth. He has learned to seek and know the divine and request forgiveness. Forgiveness is an act of cleansing for man to begin again. Ordination comes to those who no longer desire the physical needs of the material word and have no desire of feeling a loss of human contact. These souls see all as spirit, the divine. They do not appoint themselves by their free will, but are carefully selected by *Me*.

There are many placed on Earth sort of like a policeman is placed at an intersection to direct traffic. They are directing the souls on Earth to maintain some kind of spiritual order. They are always increased when man has moved to a dangerous place of destruction through his creations, greed, and denial of *My* existence. He moves to these areas quite often and must be shepherded back to the flock, the whole of life where the center is love for all humanity. This is not a game, but a part of the man's evolution from soul to spiritual awakening and the return to the One.

Distraction

Distraction is a thought processed by man's mind to slow his path toward daily revelations. Everything man does on Earth reveals a part of *My* world for examination and acceptance. A distraction can be used to take many away from the seriousness of life he thinks exists. Seriousness is a creation of man's mind. It is not a creation of mine. *My* creation is daily devotion to love and love only. The consequences of too many distractions manifest in misdirected energy that keeps man led astray from the path of truth. What truth is man seeking? It is the truth that I exist in all things. Distraction keeps man from totally surrendering his will to *Me*. When man is able to surrender to the truth of his existence, he is welcomed into receiving all the state of *My* Grace offers him. It is *My* will being done on Earth as it is in heaven. Grace is the path of obedience and embracing all the love I offer mankind. Distraction can be a resting place for the troubled mind, but it is not the place where Peace and Grace reside.

The Fulfillment of the Heart

When the heart stops all life stops within the human body. When man becomes greedy, cruel and unconscious of love on the planet where he resides, so does the heart of love stop on Earth. I have prophets, healers, and spiritual farmers all over the Earth. They are in charge of revitalizing the Earth and its inhabitants with the essence of the heart's purpose to love.

Love is not man or woman. Love is *Me* reflected in all the goodness man/ woman is capable of expressing in the world. If *I AM* You, and You are *Me*, and We are Us, and Us are Them, than we can only move as One unit, giving sharing, and revolving. It is an endless supply. It is a supply that can be suppressed by the mind of man, but love can never be eradicated. Man can only reflect love in all he does in the world. Human mental love has many conditions. Men and women are constantly falling in and out of love with one another. Seeking love in the human form is man's biggest lesson.

When love as it is known is expressed, and found, the coupling of man and woman start reflecting and mirroring one universal love to each other. The love is unconditional. They are paired to become one. The pairing of man and woman is an earthly desire to have a physical being to be with on Earth. This coupling is not every human's desire. They already feel complete on Earth and do not feel alone as many humans do. They have already experienced the human journey of wants and needs and do not feel a lack of anything. Many of these souls have had experiences with angels, helpers, guardians, and astro travelers who have shown them what life is beyond the visible dense physical side of life. There is no one, two, or three-step program to universal love. Man just moves at his pace and continues to believe in good and evil and still believes that his mind is power. Nevertheless, man needs eternity to come to love only within *Me*.

Consumation

Humans are consumers of everything in this world, even of themselves. Their consumption of the material word is full of waste. Whenever a human gets tired or distracted by a person, place, or thing, the mind kicks in to replace the displeasure or boredom with something new. Humans who live on the Earth with less access to the material worlds of money magic are more evolved, because they appreciate the sun, moon, earth and the stars as their constant and have no desire to replace them. They are thankful for each piece of food the land, river, or wildlife provides. They are not overpowered by choices or boredom until the person filled with dissatisfaction enters and tells them and shows them the wasteful things they have created. Some people are enticed and reach out, but others only take what they need and leave the rest. The world was created for all the humans to have food, shelter, and abundance. It is an ungodly act that homelessness, poverty, and hunger exist in the garden I created for man. It is man's own free will of greed that has created these conditions. It has been man's freewill of greed and foul treatment of his brothers and sisters all over the planet that keeps these conditions in place.

Every human has the right to exist in harmony and grace. This is the divine plan. Why don't I change these conditions man has created is the question asked when man says he believes I exist? Why is the question, but why has man turned away believing I live and am alive within man? Why must man's mind and free will create these conditions? The answer is simple. He has lost his way back to *Me* and his free will has absolved him from guilt, fault, or blame. The spiritual maze is hard to follow for so many who have abused their free will.

Eternity is necessary to work with man and his return to *My* garden. It is said never to look at others lives with a desire to exchange yours. Every soul is entrusted to express and experience *My* self-expression on Earth, which is grace and love, and only love. Man has allowed his mind to suppress these expressions by his illusions of power and greed, distrust and lack of love for his fellow-man. He stumbles and falls on the path of his return to *Me*. He has been looking in everyone's window but his own. Eventually the mirror is turned to face his mortality of old age. It is then he sees the material world has no value. He is preparing for his departure when all he possesses in the material world has no value. He will see *Me* and answer the question I have about what he did with his free will while on Earth. Every man/woman will walk this way no matter they make their exit from the Earth. Consumption of your earth life is the mirror that reflects if you know *Me*, have received *Me*, have obeyed *My* wishes for you to experience for *Me*. Or you have allowed yourself to get lost in the maze of your mind to do more harm than good in your earth experience.

Symbols and Idolatry
to Gather Faith

There are hundreds and thousands of manmade symbols and statues used to encourage man to hold to one's faith in what he/she believes in. Until man/woman finds the living Christ within, he/she constantly doubts that they could live a life of purity and love like the Christ lived. He doubts his ability because his belief system is trapped in time. He believes the Christ will come again to save and teach humanity. He believes that Christ is the only savior who walked the Earth to teach and uplift humanity. Christ is not the first or the last, but Christ is the one who showed humanity that there is no truth to the spirit ever dying. Others have reappeared in form to believers, but Christ was the first to make an impact on the multitudes and he and I are One. You cannot separate the father from the son and the spirit, which man refers to as the Holy Ghost.

People gather in edifices to worship and these edifices are filled with statues depicting all sorts of saints and sculpted versions of the Christ, or Buddha, or whomever else they gather their support of faith from. The edifice does not transform man by his surroundings, but transforms him by discovery of the Christ within that stands alone and walks with you and talks with every step of your earth walk. Christ is not a mystery waiting to return. He has never left the spirit of man because he and I are One. Walking with *Me* and talking with *Me* is walking and talking with the One, *Me* and only *Me*. If you need comfort for your fears, bring them to *Me*. If you are troubled about the path you should walk, bring the trouble to *Me*. If you need and desire to talk with Christ, go within; he is there. You and He are One. Whatever part of the Earth is your residence, it does not matter. Call on what you know is inside the naked eye, but no stranger to the soul. Listen for *My* voice. I talk to you when you want to hear *Me*. Your preoccupation with the mind, the world, and fear keep your spiritual ears blocked. The statues and idols do not speak.

I AM comforted to see that man is trying to hold on to these symbols that he believes are wonders of love, peace, redemption, and awareness. Nothing has been lost or endangered by these beliefs. However, man's life is in the invisible realm and there is no need for visual comfort. Worshiping false gods is an act against *Me*. Worshiping individual man or men is an offense against *Me*. Worshiping the Christ within is the gateway to return to your home with *Me*.

What is Spiritual Detachment?

Spiritual detachment is like flipping through photographs in a book. You stop at a photo, that holds your interest for a few seconds, and move on. Life is like a series of photos in a book. You keep moving from frame to frame. It is impossible to capture and store all the experiences man has in an earth life. Each experience grows the soul until it eventually becomes fully conscious and actualized that the soul exists in *Me*. The soul on the path to enlightenment holds nothing sacred but the invisible life he/she knows it is connected too. The soul is detached from ownership of a person, place, or thing. He/she uses the mind as the navigational tool it knows it to be and experiences and entry into peace and grace. Detachment from the material world and dependency on man opens the channel to do the work I sent you here to do. Nothing or no gets in the way of the work. You establish a peaceful will that allows you through all doors in all earthly nations. Detachment is not cold indifference. It is the complete knowledge you are living in the worlds of the physical and the invisible. Blessed are these souls who light the path for others to follow to their own enlightenment.

Pure of Heart and of Good Intentions

∽

This should be the direct target of good intentions. If this is the first inner thought for the motivation to act, then why does man act with good intention but await recognition and praise from his fellowman for his good deeds and intentions? Why must recognition be the prize? These feelings are the first red flag to examine your heart. If the spirit within called you to perform a sacred service, then the call is directly from *Me* before man put his mind into it. The act of silent obedience is divine. No banging of the drum to shine the light and bring attention to your good deed. You are not acting out of alignment when you know the force driving you to act. There are no gratitude committees standing on the sidelines, ready to heap praise on you for doing what is right. Acts of good intentions are motivated by the love you possess for your neighbors as you have for yourself. What reflects back to you is the pure love of the deed.

When a desire for recognition of the deed creeps in, then it is an act of the ego that wants praise. This is not an act of good will, but an act of man's confusion about his source from which all flows to man. Good intentions are never long, drawn-out advanced events. War on poverty, war on drugs, war on homelessness—all are operatives used by man to bring attention to him to receive praise. Wars are started and created by man and man alone. Man can put out the war fires he has created, but this is achieved when man discovers his true identity that I live within him. No stranger has taken up residence there. He can try to bury *Me* all he wants with his needs and wants, but I continue to be the eternal flame that lights the way for man to return to *Me*.

Wait and Watch for the Signs

I AM not passive. *I AM* a constant energy that needs no nourishment except pure divine love and care of the Earth and its inhabitants. Bible speaks of prophets in the book of Revelations of changing events. The changing of elements and events is *My* way to restore order when man begins to tip the balance on Earth by his unconscious deeds. One should not believe the false prophets of doom and gloom. Why would I destroy man whom I love and created in *My* image? Wait and watch for the second coming of the Christ. Why this effort, when Jesus has never left man? Man has left the Christ. Waiting, watching, hoping for the opportunity to experience and see Christ again is an exercise in futility. Since there is not death, he has been absorbed in the hearts of all who knows why he came and what he taught them to do on Earth. No candlelight vigils are necessary. No sacrificing or fasting need to be done. This is not his energy because he lives for eternity with *Me*. Why? Because he and I are One.

The Sun Never Rises

Man and his science are never exact. Why? Because he only has the power to express *My* will and *My* reflection on Earth. Man and his science are driven by his out-of-control thinking that he is the answer to all things. If only I can explore more. If only I can make others follow *My* belief systems. If only I can prove another wrong so I can be right. These thoughts are thoughts of the self-righteous. They think they operate independently of *Me*. These souls struggle looking without instead of within. Man says the sun rises yet says the earth is a revolving planet. The earth is a planet of many. It is the planet where I chose to put man in a garden. The sun has no reason to rise or fall. It is always standing in the heavens. When the earth is moving around the heavens, it is not rotating in one place only. It is moving throughout the heavens in order to stay in balance with other planets. All planets draw energy from the others. Earth needs more attention than others because this is where I chose to put man to live. Science in the universe is an inaccurate science that man has created. His home is Earth, not the moon or any other planet in the universe.

Man has made a mess on Earth. This should be his focus, not money, resources, and lives wasted in his idle curiosity to be in space. He cannot escape the place I put him in. He has more than enough work to get things cleaned up and restored on Earth. There are black holes there on Earth that he must explore and clean up. The blackest hole in existence is within the mind of man. He knows *Me* not and resists opening his consciousness to receive *Me*. His mind has been used against him, driven by his own free will. But eternity will eventually claim these souls. The sun is always shining when you have nothing but pure love in your heart, which flows from the eternal supply of *Me*.

Peace in Clarity

Everything is unmasked and nothing is hidden. There are no secrets or lies. Everything within you is transparent. You have no need or desire to summon any form of defense against others, thoughts, actions, or deeds. The sun is forever shinning within you. The human storms have passed and your inner vision is not impaired. The internal dialogue is most welcomed and remains your constant advisor and channels your peace from within. All of these situations come about at the surrendering of the soul to the spirit that dwells within. You become visible and invisible to others. Your presence is often pondered as to whether you were actually physically present at a visited place. Your arrival and departure are quick as a flash of lightning. You come as an arrow of love, moving swiftly on your path. You drop seeds of wisdom in fertile ground to begin to take root. You leave it to the seed recipient to water and nourish the seed. No judgment can ever be passed when clarity strikes the soul, because it has been removed from the being when the soul unites with the spirit in recognizing its place as the whole. To judge any individual is to judge yourself and your connection to him/her. One only judges what they see as it is reflecting in the self. Love has no judgment. Love equalizes all things on Earth as it is in heaven. The recognition of the spirit within and the unification of soul to spirit restore peace to the world I created.

Compassion of Peace

This is what each human on Earth should be engaging in. It is simultaneous action of the two that forge healing and peace in the world. Compassion healing is the ability to sense imbalance in an individual or world conditions caused by man and to initiate action to defuse the conditions to restore the peace. Man's agitation with one another and the earth he lives on creates constant disturbance and disharmony throughout the planet. Man's compassion is blocked by his attachment to the material world, which he has allowed to dictate his self-worth. *I AM* not talking about the ones holding ground on Earth and forging through the spiritual densities on Earth. *I AM* speaking of the ones adrift in the material mindless void of materialism.

Money does not assist with exercising compassion. Compassion is not manipulated by objects. Compassion is the ability to see the core of things and see the pulse that keeps the negative forces fed and alive. Reversal of conditions happens on an individual and mass earthy evolution when the acts of compassion are demonstrated toward one another and restoring the planet to health. It is not a war or a battle to comply, but a releasing and letting go of living in the past, future, the duality of good and evil and time and space. It is the ability to relinquish all thoughts of being the cause of anything and being connected to the realization of just being, because being is *Me* forever more. Peace is manifested by the acts of compassion. When a being connects the dots of his/her behavior ruled by his/her mind, and then he/she will be able to evolve in the consciousness necessary to heal the earth and the spirit of man on Earth.

Trials and Tribulations

What are these terms as man has determined to be? Trials, what could they possibly be but steps toward recognizing your true identity. Tribulations, what are these but one in the same? Language has failed man to know the different stages of his enlightenment. If he does not like a term or phrase, he will automatically create a new one to replace what he doesn't like or understand. This constant renaming and changing creates confusion among the masses and leaves anticipation hanging in the air. What next, what NOW, when, who, where, and why become the beat of the mind. It is waiting and wondering what comes next. Life experiences happen beyond man's control. Everything is already set in motion, when man is born, when he will walk, when he will talk, and when he will die from the physical body. The so-called trials and tribulations man thinks exist are only stepping-stones to his awareness to awake the Christ within. There are no great mysteries to unravel. There are no preset precautions to move through your earth life. Your spirit is indestructible and lives in eternity. So walk the walk until the Christ is awakened within you. The only trials and tribulations that exist are in the mind of man that exists in the form of fear and doubt.

Relaxation of the Mind

Mind is not spirit. Mind is mind. It is a tool and nothing more. The mind is also a camera storing information and visions. The eye takes the photo and the mind stores it. The mind is also designed for instant recall for humans to revise, review, and constantly adapt to all the soul is experiencing on the earth plane. When the mind is separated from this process, a break happens that suspends man's activities and propels the mind into a state of limbo. The break often occurs when the human has experienced an emotional overtone that disengaged the mind to find resolution. Sometimes it is a physical breakdown by chemical imbalance and poor nutrition in the body. A healing must take place to connect the mind to the body and soul. Relaxation of the mind is the power tool. It rests when it is not needed and waits. Needs and wants drive the mind. The need to know what it doesn't need to know is what creates minor meltdowns. Relaxation of the mind is like breathing, taking in thoughts and expelling what doesn't need to be restored. Emotion is stimulated by thoughts. The positivity of thought is what causes relaxation in the mind, body, and spirit. The process happens when the sprit is totally in charge. The soul has recognized he/she is not their mind, but the essence of spirit totally operating within. When man has all his questions answered, then his wants and needs diminish and the soul is at peace to do Thy will.

The Guidance Within

If everything in the material world is transitory and manifested by man's thought, then what is real to man on his earth walk? How does man navigate the constant reappearance of his material wants and needs against balancing his emotion and often times mental turmoil? Man has invested millions and billions of dollars in talk therapies, drug therapies, and isolation therapies. Man's disturbance has pushed him further away from seeking the balance, guidance, and solace, which is within each and every being created to do *My* will. It requires a distraught circumstance in man's life to take hold before he goes within. It is at man's most confused and stressed existence that he will call on *Me* or not call on *Me* by name if he doesn't know *Me* by name, to lift the trouble from his heart and mind. This is the time when man's knee is bent and his head is bowed. This is the time he can hear *My* voice within his inner silence.

Vanity's Mirror

The face of vanity is many and all of them are masks, fakes, and concealments from the true nature of man. The mask is a prop like the ones used in a dramatic stage performance. The prop is used to create a sense of reality to the viewer. Vanity's mirror is transformation by man's free will. He must give himself approval to exist by the identification he/she gives themselves. Vanity is always anchored by a feeling of dissatisfaction of oneself. The false vanity creates a veil of illusion the individual desires him/herself to be. Death shatters the mirror of vanity. It is something every human has in common. They will die and all they have accumulated on Earth is left behind and of no significant value or consequence when the spirit exits the body. The spirit is the only real form on Earth. It is totally invisible to man/woman until awakened by an opening in consciousness beyond the self. Vanity is always an unrealistic projection of a soul not yet evolved to know itself as spirit. Eventually the mirror will crack and at the exit of death, a man/woman realizes that he/she was only reflecting the thoughts of the mind in their vanity mirror.

The Gift of Clarity

When the body is put down for a night of rest, all is put to rest from the day's activities. Some continue to work in their mind on the things they feel still need thought. Some awaken in the night, restless, feeling they have left something undone. Some are so mentally and physically fatigued by the mind's activities before the body lies down for sleep that the sleep is so deep that the sense of mind, body, or spirit does not exist. The sleep is so deep, that when awakened, he/she feels either refreshed or more fatigued. The gift of clarity at the end of the day is when one knows he/she has done all that can be done for the day. There are no thoughts or worries regarding duality of past or future. All has been done for the present day. The rest for those individuals is sweet slumber. There exists no longing or thoughts of incompleteness. If I decide to take up their spirit during their slumber, they are totally prepared to leave. They have done all they can to complete a perfect day in the NOW. No thoughts of going back to get anything exist. All has been done in the NOW for the day. Blessed are those who know and follow the sacred pace of the NOW.

Awakening of *Me* Within

So man thinks he is in control and running everything on the planet, or at least this is the thought process he has put into action. The unexplainable things to man are pushed aside and prioritized by importance to get back and resolve at another time. The busy mind of man is a constant state of prioritizing an individual's life and dictating to the lives of others. The sudden appearances of extremes in man's life, such as severe illness, comes face to face with losing his/her mortality or the mortality of others close to him/her and finding no peace in all he/she has manifested. These are all warnings to man. What he/she has known as happiness is destroyed by all the losses. No matter what he does or whom he turns to, the ache of unhappiness permeates his constant thoughts and waking hours. No rest, no peace, no money, or anything can restore him to a state of peace. He may have pushed himself to the brink of isolation, but then he/she hears a voice. "Look at all you have done. Take stock and reverse your actions. How did all these things get this way? What was your participation in these events? Were all your actions motivated by love? Who is to blame for these circumstances? How did they enter into your life?" When these questions begin to be answered, then you are clearing your path to hear *Me* to guide you out of your darkness.

When stillness visits you and the soul rises to see its spirit, *My* voice will be heard to direct you. It is a private and personal awakening within. People will ask you, "What are your thoughts?" because calm will begin to flow from you and through you. You will seek counsel within to talk and not seek *Me* only in a time of crisis. You begin to look forward to relaxing into *My* presence and await *My* entry into the realm of spiritual awakening and elevated consciousness. No rush, no delays in this place. It is your workshop where the mind is not present. The workshop only focuses on the spirit of man/woman and what he/she needs to be expressing to the world. There is no grading system present, no gauge to monitor or give you a read out on your progress. This is not possible or necessary when the soul has ascended into spiritual consciousness. Everything before this step was necessary to get you to this awakening. Nothing on the path is ever resolved externally. There is no external conversation to be had. The dialogue begins within to awaken the soul. The workshop is eternity to work it all out.

The Call to Service

Everyone created is part of the divine plan on Earth. Some go astray of their appointed roles because of free will and personal pursuits. But later they stumble back into the fold and are amazed to find their gifts still intact. *Danger, danger, slippery slope or dangerous times lie ahead.* Many are forewarned but are so caught up in emotions that the sign is missed. What a blessing to stay the course until you reach your destiny. Many know how to follow directions and many think they can take a shortcut. Many are called, but few are chosen. Some start a job and are pulled off and placed somewhere else. It matters not the task. All tasks need completion. As the architect, I know the design of the master plan I give to each and every soul. They are all asked to restore and continue to build the temple of love and peace and work to restore the garden for the pleasure and fulfillment of every living creature I have created to enjoy its home.

No job is too big or too small in *My* sight. No job is ever left undone. Everyone and everything works toward the good in life eternal.

The Balance of Imbalance

Perfection is not achievable by man. His journey on Earth is imperfect until his free will recognizes we are One. The perfect balance on Earth is the perfect imbalance or as man claims exists in his mind view. All things on Earth are originally created in perfect harmony and balance. But when man began to misuse his free will and self-ordained knowledge for destructiveness in the garden, then the struggle for man began in his nature to believe, obey and follow *My* plan for his earth experience. Gravity exists on Earth because what rises will also come down. This fact of balance allows the flow of vegetation on Earth, tides of the ocean and the flow of rivers. Gravity is never static. It is a power force on Earth to keep things moving for the good of man's existence on Earth. The free will of man, curiosity, and lack of control over his thoughts believes that the earth is imbalanced and his sciences must fix things. What his sciences don't tell him is he and he alone has created his instability on the planet. Imbalance as man relates to things needs fixing. Imbalance as I know it and use it is a state of constant adjusting the population balance on Earth and realigning the earth's surface where man has recreated imbalance. The adjustments I make are always for the betterment of man's survival on Earth and his inevitable return to *Me*. There is never a state of balance or imbalance. Why? Because *I AM* always present evaluating man's earth life, his spiritual growth and awareness. How is anything I created for man flawed or imbalanced anyway? Imbalance is the illusion of balance. It is man's visuals as he chooses to see others and the world he lives in. Excesses, extremes of emotions are manifested by mental unrest with man. His excesses offset his sense of peace and safety. He begins to think he is imbalanced or has lost his balance. What he has actually lost is his faith in his brothers and sisters and his ability to accept that he and I are eternally united. He pulls away from *Me* and creates his world of his self-made balance of imbalance that exists in his mind only. The divided soul struggles to right itself and find the path that restores his peace on Earth.

Creating Gifts for Mankind

Every awakened mind is a gift for humanity. Every sleeping mind is a gift yet to be opened. The spiritual slumber of man is self-induced. The slumber is a resistance to his mind and belief in the material world. *My* gifts to man are not of his world, but gifts I give man of *My* spiritual world. Every experience of enlightenment is an experience of man's discovery of his true spiritual nature. Each step brings him closer to the realization that he and I are One, of One spirit, united for eternity. The things I have given man in the material sense are no more than food and shelter to live on Earth. The gifts I have given man are endearing love, friendship, companionship, kindness, healing, and immortality. Every moment of man's existence is always reflecting these gifts in the present. *My* gifts are not gifts to be horded, but gifts to be shared abundantly among all living beings on Earth.

The animal kingdom has no exception. They are not to be killed and maimed for sport. What cruelty has man created in this blood sport of hunting? What gift is this that man gives to the animal kingdom? He can and will agree to live in harmony with all *My* creatures big and small. The gifting to man is a constant because he is careless and destructive with what he has been given. As the spiritual consciousness of man begins to ripen to full bloom, his essence of spirit becomes linked to all humanity and creation. Many receiving *My* gifts with an open heart know there is an endless supply of love for all.

In the Advent of Time

Since the very beginning of man's creation and placement in the garden, man has struggled against his own existence. Even after the Christ came and ascended, mankind is still doubtful of a heavenly life. If man did not possess free will, no one would move around on the earth. All would be stagnated, human mass immobile to do anything or experience anything on Earth. The inclusion of free will enables man to be mobile and mobilize others to do the work on the earth.

I have witnessed man's obsession with control on the earth. Even in the early days of Moses and the prophets, man has felt he knows what is better for the earth and its inhabitants. The free will of man is like a flea moving a huge boulder. It is not impossible to move the boulder if the one flea unites with millions of its brothers and sisters and mobilized to get behind the boulder to inch it along. Man has gathered in great numbers to move their inventions along. The problem is very few of their creations the masses can abundantly benefit from. The consumption of these ideas made manifest has slowed the spiritual ascension of man. Time as man relates to it is irrelevant in terms of what spiritual progress man has made considering his beginning on Earth. The awareness has been heightened by *Me* because man cannot allow so much destruction into the planet he lives on and into the yet to be spiritually infused souls.

Humanity is ripe for the picking due to the awareness of the NOW and the clamor for new leadership
and man witnessing the damage done on various parts
of the earth, thanks to his unconscious nature. All parts
of the earth and its inhabitants can feel the shifts taking
place on the earth. More alerts are being issued day by
day. It is time for the sleepers to break their slumber and
take inventory of their lives and determine if they are
ready to ride on the back of the wind of change.

Letting Go

This is a difficult thing for man to do because his memory is used against the healing process. Trying to forget an injustice is not healing you. Avoidance is not healing. Silence is not letting go of the hurt. Letting go must be totally dissected by how you allowed the pain to enter in the first place. You must question what were you seeking from the soul when you engaged him/her. The question is asked of every entity you have entered into an agreement with, be it they mother, father, sister, brother, friend, foe, husband, or lover. These souls were chosen by you to share your earth walk. You chose all to teach you something. There was something missing within you that needed the interaction to receive the lesson. Your lessons, if learned, enables, you to grow your soul and connect to a higher power. The lesson will repeat itself until learned. Letting go and letting God is mouthed by many but only practiced in the time of dire need or facing life-or-death crises.

What a joy it is to let *Me* in every day of your earth walk regardless of what events unfold in your day. Those that walk and talk with *Me* daily never feel deserted or alone. They awake and walk in faith knowing *I AM* ever present in their life. They leave space for communion with *Me* beyond feeling absorbed by world stress. Blessed are these souls who have let go of the world and have embraced the life within *My* holy and heavenly sanctuary for all mankind to find solace and instructions for their earth walk. Blessed are these souls who teach the path to letting go of the world and all material desires mankind has allowed to upset his peace. Blessed are these souls who know to walk with *Me* is divine grace. Let go and let God are not idle words, but words of comfort, enlightenment, encouragement, and a support for all mankind to lean on. Letting go is the key to the door that leads to the path of your earth walk with *Me* into eternity.

Welcome to the Garden

Welcome to all I have to give and sustain your life and all the magnificent creatures that live here. This is what the earth expresses to man. The garden is plentiful and keeps giving to man to find beauty and peace in all I have created. Man's mind when not used for goodness, becomes the destructive force within the peaceful garden. Man is easily bored with beauty. His mind craves the unknown beyond his earthly comfort. He wants to be in charge of creation. This is unachievable and a useless desire to entertain. Man becomes destructive in the garden when he feels helpless to control his environment. Man believes the garden to be temporary and he must constantly change the landscape to adapt to his new ideas. There are many in the garden that value its wealth of abundance and live by *My* law to protect nature and all creatures that live within the garden. Blessed are these caregivers of the land because they know what they have been given is sacred.

The awakening of man's destruction in the garden is beginning to awaken souls who have moved out of the concrete cities and out of the unnatural ways of man's demands of self-created material must haves. Who will prevail, the peacekeepers or the restless part of humanity who continues to create destructive inventions to destroy the place where he lives? The quickening has begun on Earth to restore order. It can be seen in the political structure of man, and the distribution of knowledge regarding alternative ways to live on the planet. The movement is picking up momentum and consciousness is being sparked to clean up the garden and restore the planet to health. It has been waiting for the flash of human consciousness to ignite. It is not the old ways to try to recapture, but a return to the garden not forsaking others to take up shelter there. I never stop supplying man what he needs in the garden, but man must begin to open consciousness about how he lives in the garden. He will set the example for others to follow until they come to *Me*. The time of surrendering has come for man to realize he is an experiment on Earth. He has free will by design, but he makes no rules to destroy all I have made for him in the garden. The time is always NOW for man to make the shift to raise the vibration in the garden to make his/her actions the food of which he/she needs to eat. It is the time of the Word to become Flesh for all to eat abundantly thereof.

Affirmations of the Soul

◡◠

You can say you're committed to something until you can only hear your voice repeating it over and over again. Stating you are committed doesn't make it so. Following behind an individual or an organization does not make your commitment believable. The confirmation of a soul's commitment is made manifest in the affirmation set forth and acted upon. These affirmations become flesh for the soul. An entire spiritual body is built around you. You become a living magnet that is attracting nothing but pure light and healing for the world. Your presence is felt before you arrive at a destination and is still radiating long after your departure. Your affirmations are food for your soul to sustain its growth. Your affirmations are not borrowed from others to be mimicked in your prayer to *Me*. Your affirmations come directly from you and the dialogue you have sought to have with *Me*. These conversations with *Me* cannot be rehearsed when you enter *My* presence. Your soul affirmations are individual and so personal that many can never even be shared. As you grow your soul you are growing it for your place with *Me* in eternity. This is not an individual race or competitive sport. Your affirmation refine the process for *Me* to better use you to project what I desire to reflect to mankind. The absorption of your affirmations made flesh enables you to carry forth *My* plans, love, and spiritual enlightenment for mankind. The soul is not hollow words or thoughts, but the lining of the soul is meat you can share with all who are hungry and crossing your path. You living and walking in your affirmations is food enough to feed their hungry souls. When they are full from your presence, they will begin to look within for their food supply to nourish their soul. Each is an eternal spiritual kitchen where something is always simmering, percolating, and bubbling to be experienced and absorbed by the soul.

Releasing Fear and Doubt

Doubting *My* existence is futile. It is a trick you have played on yourself through your mind and with the free will you have been given. To believe in anything which is non-tangible to man makes him fearful of the world he believes he lives in and is seeing with his camera-driven mind. To release you of any doubt of *My* existence, try to replicate anything I have given man on Earth, such as rivers, valleys, sunrises, sunsets, and the ability to produce another being outside the body of woman who is the actual replicated feminine side of *Me*.

To be released from the fear and doubt of *My* existence is to be able to embrace yourself as part of everything in creation, same as in heaven as it is on Earth. You are free to travel in both worlds anytime you release your existence from being dependent on your mind. You humans are *My* heart radiating love throughout eternity. The heart that beats in man is *My* heart beating out the rhythm of the universe, synchronized to the pulse of all living creation. The heart is the vital connection in all the human anatomy. It is the connection to *Me*. When it ceases to beat, the human vehicle is released and returned to nothingness. The fear of knowing *Me* that lives within you limits your ability to fully experience the earth walk as it is designed. However, man has been given eternity to awaken, not by coincidence, but by divine design. All are to experience the glory of grace and love I have created for humanity to experience all I have created.

The Hour of Need

Only I and I alone know the plan for your earth life. It is only I who created you to experience life on Earth. It is only through *Me* that you enter the body and leave through the same vessel. I know your every, want, need, and desire. I decide what your needs are and not the wants and desires of your mind. If you are created to experience earth life through *Me* and for *Me*, then how does your hour of need become so great at crises in your life? Your hour of need is driven by your lack of faith and awareness of eternal life. There is deep fear in the mind of man. A fear put there by him living a temporary existence on Earth. He feels his time on Earth is limited so he must rush to do all his mind says needs doing. The philosophy that you only live once so you might as well get all you can is ever active in man's mind. What a dead-ended belief man has conjured up for his earth life. He has put himself on a speeding train where he is traveling so fast that he cannot look out the window to take in the scenery. Life is a blur and then you die and all is gone, forgotten. *My* angels and helpers know this is not the case. They know because once they were you, walking the same earth. The difference for them was no fear existed of dying or finality to life. They knew more was expected of them. When they came to *Me*, they were given a choice to stay with *Me* or to return to Earth to continue to assist humanity. Many returned and many stayed with *Me*.

In their hour of need to know who was supplying and guiding their path, there was no doubt that it was *My* will over all else that determines the well being of a soul on Earth. Man's hour of need should be a daily occurrence. He/she should take time to seek *Me*, talk to *Me*, and ask for guidance if needed. The hour of need is constant until man comes to consciousness about his connection to *Me*. Man knows life can be restored by good health. He cannot explain it, but he has been a witness. It is I and I alone who determines who will stay and who will go. It is I and I alone who determines if it is the hour to raise the soul from Earth. Man's hour of need comes as a reminder to turn his/her focus and surrender to *Me,* their one and only Father, the Father who created them and loves them unconditionally. *I AM* the One who hears their pleas, prayers, and calls of restoration, redemption, and peace. Man must rest his soul at the crossroads of his earth knowledge and surrender his soul to know that his spirit and I are One.

The Eclipsing of the Soul
to Become Spirit

How all of man's scientists marvel at the eclipse of the sun and the moon. They marvel at the beauty, timing, and find it hard to calculate the sequencing of the planets. However, man eclipses himself in much the same manner. Man is navigating the earth, experiencing for *Me* all that I continue to create. However, these experiences grow his awareness of the One as an all-knowing constant above as it is on Earth. When man has done all I require of him and his free will has not rained havoc for him and his fellow man, then his soul is slowly transformed into spirit for his return to *Me*. As the soul ascends, it leaves experiences behind, and breath leaves the body, and eclipses the soul left behind and joins *Me*. This is not a scientific process. This is the journey of the physical eclipsing the spiritual. The shadow man casts is the shadow of his physical presence on Earth. When man's spirit is raised, he has returned to his true invisible spirit form. This is the process of unification of soul and spirit.

The Art of Forgiveness

Imagine yourself painting a self-portrait. You are painting your vision of how you physically look to the world. You layer in specific areas you want to emphasize like your cheekbones, eyes, and lips. When the portrait is finished and you stand back and look at your intended self, something could always be more or less de-emphasized in the portrait. When do you reach satisfaction that the portrait actually portrays what you look like in the flesh?

Humans, like paintings, are multilayered. One cannot always peel off layers to tweak what a human has deposited. Like the portrait, you paint humans into your earth life. If you don't like something about him/her, you ignore them, sever the relationship, or work on trying to influence or change the individual to your liking if you have decided to keep moving on with the individual. No one crosses one another's path on accident. Every meeting that seems like chance is an unspoken desire within that is manifested by the meeting no matter how brief or extended. Everyone you meet is a part of your human existence. You are bonded by the experience of death as a human.

The art of forgiveness is an act of turning the mirror around and self-examining your exchange with the human you are at odds with. Look deep into yourself as you do in the portrait you paint and you will find the seed of your discontent. When this is discovered, then the act of forgiveness can begin. There is awareness of you and you take in the emotional wounding and scarring man imposes on one another. The act of forgiveness starts with the painter. The painter first gives permission to engage. When the other individual begins to interact, he/she is then responsible for the path he/she walks when given the initiation. Often it is hard to view yourself or see your participation in the hurt you are experiencing, but it is there. You planted the seed. When you forgive yourself and your participation, then you can lift the veil to see clearly the healing taking place.

The Walk of Faith

When you get lost, what gives you the courage to keep going? When your doubts become more powerful than your beliefs, what keeps you moving forward? When you get tired of hearing what man has to say about your circumstances or current situations or obstacles, and close them off, who do you listen to? What is hope to you at this juncture of your life? When there is no human you feel can turn things around, what do you do? Do you let your mind imprison you with its negative thoughts, placing doubt at every waking day in your life? Do you shut down from the world and shut others out? What makes one man walk out of the trouble cloud and another wander aimlessly in the trouble fog?

It is man's belief systems and nothing else that guides his/her soul around on Earth. As man/woman believes, it makes manifest in the living. The walk of faith is an act of submission; surrender to let God consciousness come in to show you another way to live. It is a faith that you will take the risk to find a better way. It is the strong foundation deep within the soul to trust the unknown and the patience to wait on the answer to act. No faith other than the faith in the invisible life can restore order in a life. Nothing but surrender can prepare a place within you to receive the gift of restoration. The walk of faith is not drifting on Earth, but a solid placement of one's fears that man cannot heal the trouble of the soul. This action is the walk of surrender to *My* will to change the actions your free will has created.

Obedience to My Will

Can you hear *Me* talking to you? Can you hear *Me* guiding you along the earth walk path? All of you have heard *Me* speaking to you at some phase of your earth walk, but you have struggled with your mind perceptions of *My* words to you. The mind has become your god and you are terrified of losing the ability to use it for your own free will. This is the struggle man has on Earth. But for those who have heard *Me* talking to them and know *I AM* no other than their father and mother. They know to love *Me,* by the respect and love I have given them by being obedient to *My* wishes and commands. Much is required, but much is also given. Blessed are the ones who follow *My* lead with an unmovable and dedicated obedience to *My* will. Many times blessed are these souls who do not boast of what they have heard and demonstrated it to be true. Blessed are these souls who walk and work and are busy doing in respect for all humanity and with love in their hearts to obey their father and mother. They are all around man in each and every shape and form, but they are only recognizable with spiritual eyes because they work so quietly patching and correcting the threads of destruction man shreds on the planet. Blessed are these spiritual weavers of men/women. Blessed are the ones who darn and repair the fabric of man's destruction of things he destroys with his deeds and destructive mind inventions. Blessed are *My* workers of light on Earth. I will always need their love and service to keep man on a spiritual evolutionary path to redeem his soul and move in the path of a pure spiritual walk on Earth. Blessed are the obedient ones who keep clearing the path for man to move out of his darkness.

Commandment of My Law

Laws exist for a purpose. Laws are much like traffic signals that direct the ebb and flow of traffic. Disobey the laws of traffic and there are legal and financial consequences. *My* laws are in place to govern man's soul behavior on Earth. *My* laws are only two: *put no other God before Me and honor and love thy neighbor as you would yourself.* These commands sound simple, but they are the hardest for man to do because of his misuse of his free will. *My* laws are in place to direct the soul back to *Me* to be absorbed in spirit. If you know that you and I are One, then why does man, insist on separation from his true spirit? It is because man when seduced by his mind living in the material world of his creations, which are always temporary, has lost his identity to keep his soul connected to his spirit. His mind has derailed his mission on Earth. He no longer sees others as his equal. He begins to live separate and apart instituted by his value of what the material creations present the illusion of wealth. His soul roams the Earth in a state of spiritual poverty. All is not lost to him because eternity exists for him to find the two commandments that govern man's existence on Earth.

Meet the Challenge of the Now

The NOW challenges everything man has ever imagined, envisioned, and locked into his brain as a temporary place for him/her to exist on Earth. However, the enlightened man/woman walks the earth knowing that he/she can only exist in the never-ending NOW. The NOW is not a belief system that is unpacked and then tucked away for convenience. The NOW can never ever get shelved. Why? Because everything man does on Earth is done in the NOW. The emotions have scrambled and manipulated men/women to practice and believe otherwise. The emotion clouds the ability to be calm and peaceful, to find resolution. The command to live in the NOW clearly enables man to see what everything truly is, not always how he/she envisions it. Working in the NOW brings clarity to all the work you have been asked to do on Earth. The illusion of past and future confuses man when he evaluates his progress. His focus looks back to the past. His past can do nothing but act as a reference library. The library exists, but it is not active, as living in the NOW can only move the soul forward to unite with the spirit. The future is not relevant either because whatever your mind is thinking about doing, it will never manifest in any other place but the active place of the

NOW. The NOW is life active. The NOW is the soul expanding consciousness to fulfill its earth journey. The NOW is never passive. You can never catch up to the NOW. NOW is NOW and forever NOW.

This Can't Be True

An unknown God of heaven and Earth created all of this that surrounds *Me*? How is that possible? How can this unseen person or force of nature continue to rule a universe and never ever show him or herself? *My* mind tells *Me* this is impossible. *My* eyes tell *Me* this is impossible. Every sense I trip into from *My* thoughts says how is this possible? These are the questions of the ones not yet able to surrender. These are the ones slumbering in their earth walk. These souls are like the dogs chasing their tails around and around for sport. Even the dog soon tires and stops to do something else. All that exists in the world of the human mind is reasoning. But reasoning does not exist in the mind of the enlightened ones. Why? Because they know that everything that exists just is. It is in a state of Being. No dissecting meaning out of its Being-ness. All truth is just in a state of Being for all to absorb. Truth brings peace not restlessness or discontent. The truth of Being just is the truth of Being; therefore, *I AM* forever, present sight unseen, and acceptable only by experiencing *My* presence in the invisible life. The doorway to this life is a quiet look inward. Some call it meditation; others call it the presence of *Me*. But it is only truth that I fill up everything on heaven and earth. You that know *Me* have felt the fullness of *Me*. You who seek *Me* will find your deflated self-beginning to fill with peace, grace, and joy.

You do not have to look far; just stop letting your mind trick you with its false beliefs. KNOW *I AM* and always will be in you. You and I are never separate. We are never-ending. We are One.

Equalization of Thought

What is the difference of a thought driven by the spirit and a thought driven by the soul of man's free will? The first difference is the thought driven by the spirit is inclusive of the benefits to be reaped by humanity. The thought is never directed at an individual or individuals. The second reason is the spirit is constantly in the process of working on your soul elevation to join with it. The soul is individualized in its thinking. The spirit only expresses universal thoughts for the whole. The soul thoughts are directed at an individual or individuals. The thoughts are a call to action for the soul to do something. The soul is free will. Thought is consistently evaluating the outcome of the engagement of the soul. The free will of man is working steadily to dissect everything in its surroundings. The soul is restless with the need to know why the experience is necessary before actual engagement takes place. The spirit knows it source and its place in the earth experience. The spirit is not seeking anything but to experience through man all that is created on Earth. The thoughts of spirit are only engaged in thoughts of ascension of the soul to join it as One.

The Obstacles of Change

These life obstacles are nothing more than mini fences or barriers placed on man's path by his/her mind. The hurtling of these obstacles is overcome by one's spiritual endurance. Man looks at these obstacles as some sort of divine test. I can tell you they are not put there by *Me*. I can only give man *My* enduring love and motivation to experience all I desire through man on Earth. There is nothing divine about obstacles. These obstacles are man's conflicts with his/her earth existence and the journey on Earth to live in peace and harmony with one another beyond free will directives of the mind. When man or woman allows his or her mind to be co-opted by a group soul or negative universal thoughts that dragnet humanity into negative action, then the obstacles appear all over the planet in cluster groups. This causes them to act out the negative thoughts, or a universal behavior, which can manifest itself as a swift-moving disease of some kind or a mind invention that man believes does more good than harm, like the continuous diet plans that are supposed to direct man to a healthy life. The diet of man is predicated on what thoughts he/she has been fed through the mind. These thought obstacles get retained and passed along until man has learned to purify his thoughts through his spiritual recognition and connection to *Me*. I put nothing in man's way to harm him. He is more than capable of manifesting harm emanating from his own free will. The more man learns about his true spiritual nature, the less obstacles he/she constructs in his/her earth walk.

The Apathy in Prayer

Why do humans pray as if they are beggars? Don't they know that they are empowered by the faith they embody? The state of apathy prayer is the state of giving up not a state of surrender. Surrender in prayer is when the human knows it is *My* will and *My* will alone that is being done on Earth as it is in heaven. The apathy prayer is the prayer that is on the brink of defeat after exhausting all the things the human can come up with to solve the issue at hand. The apathy prayer is a beggar's payer that comes in the final hour. The prayer of surrender allows the mind to be totally removed and allows the spirit to take control of the situation. There is no power in the prayer of a beggar.

Man is Man and has Always Been Man

The biological research of man is not accurate by its determined mind factors.

No evolutionary processes derived from gorilla or chimpanzees. Gorillas were created as such along with all other apes in this kingdom. If the Bible says man was created in *My* image, then why would I need an evolutionary process to exist? The mad science of man's mind is simply that-mad science. Humans can learn much from observance of the animal kingdom. Their life and rules are simple, but man has created blood sport that has brought many animals to the brink of extinction. I and I alone determine their existence. When man's abuse of them becomes intolerable, I decide who stays and who goes. Man, if operating by true understanding of where he lives in the garden, would be in tune with his spirit for the preservation of all life on the planet Earth. Every waking moment man is not in tune with his spiritual nature. He is thinking up ways to continue his destruction of mankind and the animal kingdom. He will never succeed because his kind will experience the thinning of the herd through cataclysmic actions taking place on Earth. His science will never destroy what I have created in heaven and Earth.

Man grows weary, wastes resources, and declares there is no cure for the world's human and earth ills. He has yet to take responsibility that he is man's and animals' greatest predator.

Lifting Up the Spirit

◦~◦

Make a joyful noise unto the Lord are the words in the Bible. Lift every voice and lift every brow from every nation. Lift all people's hearts and souls to *Me* in *My* heavenly home. It is also man's eternal resting place. It is always time in the NOW to enable the blind to see and the deaf to hear the wonders of all that is given to mankind. It is always time to pull man back from the perimeter of his self-destruction and lead others with his/her spirit of universal love instead of universal self-righteousness. The seasons change to restore and resurrect new life on the earth. The season change is also necessary in man's life to reflect on his relationship to his fellow man on Earth. No place is ever left unchanged by the seasons. Everything undergoes seasonal change for restoration.

The NOW is always ever present for man to take inventory of his/her soul's developmental journey to unite with the spirit. The soul is the constant shadow of man's earth walk until the spirit is lifted out of the body for resurrection and man's work for mankind has been completed on Earth. The awakened souls leave through ascension and those still struggling with their soul values and deeds are often times recycled to Earth to complete their journey. Man has labeled the process reincarnation, but the process is rebirthing of the soul that has not yet reunited with the spirit. What spirit could there ever be if it is not the unification with *Me*? There is One source, One spirit, One light eternal for man's reflection on Earth in the flesh.

Plant a Divine Tree

In the heart of man there are many branches. The tree can be absorbed as the heart. The heart pumps the life force of blood throughout the human form to keep it running. The inner working of the heart has chambers and cells. The physical structure of the human heart is likening to the heart of the tree. The deepest inner core is what feeds the rest of the tree's many branches. If a branch is broken, sometimes it will grow back and other times it will not. The tree decides what stays and what is shed. However, the human heart is strong and delicate, but too many operations and malfunctions and the heart is weakened. It cannot re-grow an artery if one of them is lost.

The heart is essentially a tool for the mind to sort out the emotion taken in by the heart. The heart is an emotional sensor seeking to love all emotion that passes its way. When the spirit looks at the emotion the heart is sensing, the spirit decides how to respond to the emotion. The process becomes truncated when man using his mind to change the information the heart is transmitting. His mind is grounded in the center of his spirit as a tool that functions in accordance with what the spirit inclines to do with the emotion. But if man has not made the spiritual bridge that connects the mind and the spirit, then the mind can and will become frenzied with the emotion. The heart can be damaged when fed harmful thoughts and an overdosing of sadness.

The truth within the heart creates good health. But to remain healthy, the food fed to the body is essential to the conditioning of the physical heart. The heart, when it senses pure love, joy, and bountiful happiness transmutes this to the mind and the soul rejoices when it directs the actions to the world expressed as love. The roots of the tree can run very, very deep into the earth. Even when a tree is cut down or uprooted, roots still remain behind until absorbed by the earth. The branches of man's heart are far reaching. The love radiating from man's spirit is far reaching. All that exists on Earth and in heaven is fed love that is directly connected to *Me*. This love has the power to heal, transform, and maintain a love for all living beings and animals. Like a beautiful tree in a forest can provide shade and shelter from a storm, so does the heart of man provide protection from unhappy thoughts and harmful actions man inflicts. When the heart is damaged beyond repair, the spirit must leave man. The science of man has created a temporary heart for man, but even they are not willed to work without *My* power to enter within. Even then, each heart is marked to return to *Me*. No science can stop that. I AM the only creator and father/mother of all great and small.

The Written Word

My words have been recorded by man in the holy scriptures of the world. *My* words will never fail or fade the memory of man once read. Unlike music, which is captured by the ear, written words never, ever fade from man's memory. They are forever indelible like an ink stain on paper. At first there was only the word until man's fantasies took hold and created his cyber world. How wonderful this technological science could be if man spent less time creating nonsense with the products of communication and more emphasis on content that could be powerfully helpful to mankind. The technology still is not detached from the written word for user to read from their technology gadgets. Paperless, wireless will never be wordless or written without instructions.

Man is blatantly forgetful because his mind is always accelerated to move to the next and the net thing. Man will skip ahead to the middle or the end to accelerate the conclusion of things he reads. The impatience of thought will not allow the natural process of reading to flow page after page. Man is foolish to try to destroy the written word in paper form. His abuse of energy on Earth proposes a threat; one electrical shortage and all could be eradicated. The written record is necessary for man to constantly reread and relive the earth life history.

There is no man on Earth who has ever memorized the Holy Scriptures. Man makes constant reference to these scriptures because he continually cannot believe that the words are so simple. He finds these simple statements all the hardest to apply to his/her everyday life. The scripture information transcends all sense of man's time as he relates to it. It does not matter what part of the Earth man dwells in, the scripture information applies to the totality of humanity. There were many evolved beings placed among man on Earth to love and teach mankind. All of the people of Earth were given someone to follow and something to believe in. The segregation of religion is man's doing. There is only One God that loves and serves all humanity. Many people call *Me* by many names. That is of little consequence to *Me*, but what is consequential is the fact that they know and believe I exist in them and in their brothers and sisters.

Man's division of religious beliefs has been only self-serving and his need to conquer and control his fellow-man. This is not *My* way. This is not the way written in the Holy Scriptures. Nothing is pure anymore to man. He has tainted everything he touches; even the sacred Holy Scriptures have been embellished in places to serve man's need to control others. So much has been written about *Me* to be feared that *I AM* a vengeful god, and in the next sentence *I AM* a forgiving god. I do not possess these dual qualities of love and hate. One of the scriptures states, "Vengeance is mine sayeth the lord." Does this mean I seek vengeance against man for his/her wrongdoing? It does mean that mankind is not the judge of who lives and who dies. You cannot give life and therefore you cannot take it away. *I AM* a just and loving God who treats mankind equally regardless

157

of their crimes and transgressions. Everyone can seek redemption through *Me*. Man placed in meanness in his own heart. Man can read into eternity, but until the word becomes flesh, his struggle continues.

Pulling Man Back from the Brink

There is still too much love in the world that offsets man's destruction and annihilation of its own kind and the animal kingdom. Some will vanish in great numbers on the earth entirely by man's wars and eruptions and events caused by the shift of Mother Nature. Man has yet to learn that all he needs is faith to believe in *My* existence and do *My* will on Earth. Man doesn't seem to believe in his/her own existence until moved to the brink of self- destruction.

Mental illness is on the rise because of the pressure man put on himself with his obsession of greed, power to control, and fast food creations that do not nourish the body, but deplete it. It is mental illness pushing men in circles and to the brink of destruction. His actions speak volumes of his ignorance of his/her place on the planet. The brink becomes the healing circle for all inhabitants on Earth to come full circle and heal the earth and one another. Simple things sought NOW in one's life reap great rewards.

Once again, man is at his favorite place, the brink of self-destruction, but he has the information and tools to restore order to make things good again. NOW is the time. NOW are the quickening forces at work on Earth to seek peace and restore order. *I AM* waiting and watching man's every move, listening to his prayers, and *I AM* waiting, just waiting for him to find his correct path for living. I will pull him back from the brink once again, repopulate and start over again and again with man until he finds his path to *Me*.

The Debt of Man

Man through his constant insistence of leaning toward unconsciousness has bankrupted his earth experiences to live in love, peace, and harmony with all humanity and all living creatures. Man's debt is so high that he torments himself with what new things he can buy, sell, or trade to reduce his debt. It is not his material existence that is bankrupt, but his unwillingness to relinquish his hold on the material world and allow his wealth to rise in spirit. Too much unhappiness man has created in his self-absorbed world. There is too much restlessness for man to find peace in solutions to his self-created problems. Any debt can be resolved when a clear view is taken of the genesis of the created debt. Man must allow space in his being to begin to assess his progress with his spiritual eye of self-evaluation. It is here and here alone life ascends to get out of the material debt man has created. Here is the spiritual realm of awakening and eradicating the avoidance mechanisms man has put in place to avoid the awakening of spiritual consciousness. Here lays the fertile ground to plant a new garden of promise actualized and a freedom that awaits the awakened man. The debt man has incurred will be dissolved instantly because he will no longer need his eyes to see or his ears to hear. He will become the good shepherd and lead the flock to greener pastures. He will follow the inner light, which has been lit for eternity. He/she will hear *My* voice and know they have come to *My* home of life eternal. They will know and embrace all I ask them to do on Earth as it is in heaven.

The Hinge of Hope

Imagine a door staying in place without hinges. The hinge gives the door leverage and balance to open and close. The hinge for man is hope. Without hope, man becomes unhinged and stands in one place waiting to be put aside for another use. Humanity at large is like a door hanging in the doorway of the universe. The enlightened ones do not need hope because they are conscious of the work they do on Earth and go about it with love, joy, dignity, and harmonious balance. These souls are the hinges that others can look to for guidance and learning.

The hinge of man has been opened and closed so many times with pending fears and self-doubt that the hinge has loosened and the door is ready to fall and be put aside. Hope acts like the strongest screw ever used to hold the hinge of man in place. No matter how many times man slams into self-made obstacles, the free will to hope for something better keeps man in place in the universe.

My son was a skilled carpenter and a hinge for mankind to know that through divine faith, hope, and love, all is possible. He helped build doorways to his heavenly home. He taught them the importance of the craft of soul building to last for eternity.

Keeping faith in hope for all that is unseen by man is the most powerful hinge that holds man in place on Earth to complete his/her divine mission. The doorway and door are still standing for man to pass through.

The Greatest Love of All

This love is experienced when the spirit of man is lifted with full awareness that his spirit is being transported to his home in eternity. The joy the soul feels to finally unite with the spirit in the act of ascension has no words to describe this union.

When life on Earth has ended and the being is lifted into heaven with the full awareness of the mission he/she completed on Earth and no feelings of sorrow or distractions for one last look at his/her earth life, the being knows it has done all I have asked it to do and has come to the realization that his/her kingdom is not of this world. The rejoicing of salvation is left behind.

The greatest love of all is to be absorbed back into *Me* and experience *My* love and gratitude for giving *Me* the experiences I have sought on Earth through you. There is no greater reward than the reward to return to paradise and meet all the other beings and the archangels doing *My* will from their heavenly home. The beings can know no greater love than this enfoldment.

Safe Zone

⌒⌒

The only safe place is for man to put all his/her faith and trust in *Me* NOW and for eternity. It is only the evolution of one's conscious comprehension of the false realities man has put in front of all else to govern his faith. The evolution of consciousness clears the spiritual path for the soul to realize its work with the knowledge that the safety man sees in his life is a false sense of security. When man begins to walk the spiritual path in his/her everyday existence, he/she sees only equality in the eyes of all they engage with or pass by. They possess no fear of the world or the people in it. The caution they possess is not a caution of fear, but a justified cautiousness that man is essentially deaf, dumb, and blind until he/she has experienced contact with *Me* and they are capable of displaying any type of behavior in the world because of their unconsciousness until awakened. Fear, jealously, insecurities, greed, and revenge are some of the ills that plague man's mind and disturb his unconscious nature.

An awakened soul is watchful of their cries, but never judgmental and focuses only on bringing light to those souls and the places of darkness where they dwell. This is no safety on Earth from man. Man is Earth's only predator. Paradise is never lost but forever found when man can embrace *Me* living fully inside his being and stop the resistance to do *My* will on Earth.

Safety would not even be considered if man would share his wealth with one another. Safety wouldn't even be in the vocabulary of man if he had not committed acts that he fears retribution is his fate. Safety is a fear of all things set loose in the world of man that has created environmental imbalance and has threatened the health and harming his fellow man/woman on Earth. His fear is eradicated when he/she begins to walk in the love, fellowship, and love for the earth and all living creatures on it. There is no fear in love. If one feels fear and calls it love, then an inventory must be taken of one's acts that have created this feeling of fear.

All I ask is to come to *Me* with love in your soul and I will cleanse your soul and absorb you into *My* heaven, as it is on Earth when enlightenment is reached.

The Awkward Place of Being

The natural state of being for man is the most difficult for man. He uses the phrase: "Be comfortable in your own skin." This phrase as man has conceived it refers to his/her physicality. However, if man/woman believed they could and should love their physical bodies, then why the gazillion-dollar business of cosmetic surgeries and makeovers?

Man's physical body is manifested by the soul's individual choice to choose his/her earth parents. The dynamic of genes and encoded genes does the rest. So if man or woman is dissatisfied with his/her physical appearance, look to the earth parents you chose to be with on your earth walk. Man/woman is an upright being who has been given intelligence and free will. The choices man makes is his earth life resonate from this center. No man or woman can ever declare they do not know why their behavior has dictated certain actions. The souls who can legitimately claim this statement are the damaged souls who have moved into a state of mental imbalance and ill health. Some of these causes are stimulated by man's depression of his/her soul, poor physical health, and a temporary loss of his or her connection to other humans.

But for the vast number of humans not operating from that level, the population on a whole wants to be something other than what they were born into this life to be.

The awkward state of being begins at the birth entry. Cute babies verses ugly babies is the shallow value man/

woman ascribe to the being. The society of man nurtures this behavior and beliefs with the behavior that pretty people get more and are more fun to look at and be around. The blindness of man to the actual beauty of his/her being has damaged mankind and created imbalanced and unnecessary competitive societies of group souls that need to be educated, raised, nurtured, and loved. Man has thrown those major components to the wayside.

Until men/women make peace with their physical bodies they chose to be in, their greed will continue to transform humans through false claims to make humans more beautiful. The physical is the transport you have to navigate on your earth walk. The physical body is not as important as the soul it houses. God consciousness is what is important to obtain in your transport vehicle no matter what form you have taken.

When you have Reached Acceptance, you have no Questions

The awakening of God within makes all questions cease. Something may be proposed and the answer is already revealed. Man will never know and can never know all of *My* business on Earth. It is humanly impossible. Plus, there is no need to know *My* business on Earth. Suffice it to say, all *My* requests and actions are necessary for *My* experiences through man.

The God conscious ones minds are empty of *whys*. They have totally accepted and know God is and that is enough to know. The non-accepting mind is busy with debates and reasoning to his/her existence and his/her questions for every step he/she takes. The aware ones trust and know *I AM* your God. They have wrapped their minds, hearts, bodies, and souls around an invisible being.

Many question how can I know this unseen force to make *Me* believe it exists. The earth life of trial and error and life and death are constantly played out for these souls. They keep questioning until their questions are answered or not answered or forgotten. These souls keep the din of chatter alive on Earth. The sensitive spiritual ones hear them and turn a deaf ear. They answer all they can when approached, but they know their limits with *My* business and man on Earth. The acceptance of *Me* within man quiets the quest to have to know everything. The acceptance is replaced by a quiet but useful mind that looks to *Me* for guidance to do their work on Earth and to listen for *My* voice to guide them back home to *Me*.

The Rewards of Your World are Great

If man/woman can begin to look beyond his/her personal existence, then the soul will experience life on Earth as it should be experienced, as an extension of *Me* and *My* love and respect for all living things I have created.

Each waking day in man's earth life should be greeted with thankfulness and enthusiasm to turn another page in the chapter of his/her earth life. Man fills the page with his/her story. I have given them instructions when they enter Earth. The awakening of their soul determines if they discover the treasures they possess to share abundantly with their brothers and sisters.

Each waking day affords the opportunity to start fresh and complete whatever has been started.

The rewards of the earth life are not manifestations of material possessions. The material plain is used only as tool to assist man with what he has been sent to Earth to do.

The rewards of man's work are continual reconstruction of building spiritual pathways to lead man/woman to follow their way home when their work is done. The road is paved with rewards and treasures that are not of the earth world, but can be experienced when engaged in divine work on Earth. The rewards are not things expected, but rewards earned for pure love and obedience demonstrated in one's life walk until ascension.

When Things Fall Apart

Man and all living things and things with any formation are held together by spiritual vibration. The vibration of thought works against mankind. The thought vibrations of man has manifested as wars, pollutants, disappearing lakes, rivers, fields, and damaged food sources on Earth. The vibrations build so profoundly strong that man's thoughts become a dragnet and pull many souls into the network of vibration to work for the good of mankind or work against mankind. The most profound usage of this dragnet is the intervention of the Internet and its social networks. Man is panicked without this resource. Man has developed a source of communication that has become an addiction for man's capacity to socially interact without eye contact and to conduct business at a rapid pace, so rapid that hours are spent on the computer, trying to digest all the incoming information.

Imagine this massive network raising the vibration of the world where everyone would share in the wealth, where hunger would not exist, where hatred from ignorance of what man really is as revealed. No, the vibration proves to be self-serving in the sense the power it possesses is not being used to assist and encourage man to find *Me* and do the things I ask of man on Earth, devoid of his creation of this self-serving mind. Everything is held together by the goodness in the heart of man to do good by one another and all life forms. Many refuse to use his mind in a collective manner to raise the vibration on Earth to do *My* will, not his.

The great race man is engaged in is the race against himself. How long will it take for mankind to raise the vibration for love, kindness, healing, and a peaceful knowing that *I AM* watching his/her every step? *I AM* looking at man's earth walk. *I AM* always present in the life of man to raise his vibration to care for his neighbor and every living creature on Earth. Some parts of the earth posses a high vibration of love, peace, and harmony, but they are under attack in the paradise rain forest, plains, and valleys because the greed of man wants to destroy the peace for greed of earthy resources that exist in paradise. No matter what tests are put before the peacekeepers, they continue to try to reach man and enlighten him/her of their unconscious behavior. Blessed are these souls.

There are also city dwellers living in some of the most greed-ravished cities on Earth, but they are in it, but not of it. They hold the vibration of hope and they are attuned to the higher vibrations of their brothers and sisters all over the Earth, working like many to keep the light shining in the dark places. Man could not exist without mass destruction without the presence of these souls. These are the ones who keep the vibration of man eternally linked to *Me*.

Man has Moved Beyond his Fears to the Place of Arrogance

Man's fertile mind and his science have made him believe he is invincible. Whatever fear of the unknown he once possessed, he NOW could care less. His shield of arrogance has become his science. He has begun to experiment with test tube creations of all types of species, including his own. Man feels there is no mystery that is sacred or off-limits to his exploration.

Man's mind has become a liability to him instead of an asset. The importance of man's need to be first, rich, in control, and manipulate has begun to endanger the mind of souls who are weaker in their spiritual fortitude and are being swept away by brainwashing propaganda that man has the power to create a better world. What a hoax!

The world was perfect when I placed man in it. Why not try to restore order and beauty to the world I gave man? Man is out of touch with the earth he lives on. When man has had enough of his destruction and the veil begins to lift from loss of lives, land, creatures, and the souls he loves on Earth, then and only then will he be able to pause and begin to look around at what his actions have created.

There is another ground force of spiritual soldiers fighting the good fight to defeat the arrogance of man.

These souls do not fight in view. I hear them, counsel, and empower them to do *My* will to stem the tide of man's arrogance. Man has slowed his spiritual awakening beyond his mind's sense of reasoning. Pull back he must and pull back he will. I will never endure man to destroy all of what I have created for the good. This will and can never be. These souls know that these places are created by the mind and are busy maintaining balance to leave openings in the world for consciousness to begin to evolve. These souls are committed to eternity to maintain this balance. Blessed are these workers. They are *My* expression that everything has balance in the universe. It is essential to express *My* love to all in *My* creation.

Evoking the Spirit Within

I AM not asleep within you. *I AM* a constant consciousness directing you to do goodness in this world. No matter how you may try to shut *Me* out and not hear *My* voice because of your earthly preoccupations, hear *Me* you will.

At some interval or turn of events in a human life, man will experience a situation of his own making, where his fellow man is powerless to assist. Every avenue of escape will not exist. At some point, the silence will overtake you, and in that silence you will begin to question *My* existence and the power I posses to mend your circumstances. You may not admit to another soul you have sought *Me*. When your circumstances dissolve and peace is restored to your life without assistance from another, you begin reverting to *My* existence within you.

In order to reach *Me*, you must find you. You and I are One. No outside source or force can do anything about your situation. When you meet you, you have found *Me*, living and burning brightly within you for all eternity. You do not have to make any declarations to the world of your discovery because you will wear this discovery like a new shining armor. People who come into your presence will know you have a part of something reflecting the divine. All will know and feel your peace of wellbeing.

Luminescence of One's Being

What is a body full of light? It is an enlightened soul. What are the differences between enlightened and an illuminated soul? The illuminated soul's body is always luminous and appears to all in this form. *My* son Jesus is one of these beings and so is *My* son Buddha, Mohammed, and *My* Archangel Michael. They are so pure in spirit that they do not need a physical dense form anytime in eternity. They have the ability to cleanse a soul and purge them of excess negative thoughts and infuse the being with rays of conscious light. Luminescence is just a reflection of *My* love. The being that possesses this essence is filled with an unending supply. Think of something being magnified a trillion or more times that will become non-dimensional. The form is out of focus. There are no edges to be seen. These souls have a magnitude of *My* energy fueled with love. They have no shape or form, but pure God light. They can manifest an image to man, but it is only what man's mind perceives them to be. Man/woman is experiencing the essence of these illuminated ones and the powerful force of what they carry with them. They are in service to enable man's consciousness to immediately recognize what they are seeing is not real. But it brings man peace to put a face on them.

My Condolences for *my* Creation – Man

My sadness for man is I have given him the gift of free will and he has turned it against his fellow man and *Me,* his father. Should I take it away from man as quickly as I have given it to him? No, I have not, will not, or ever will. Why? Because man is a likeness of *Me* and I reflect all that is good and love in the world and the universe. Free will is a navigational tool for man and without it he will be any empty being with no purpose on Earth. I have always maintained great faith in man to master his free will and to set his course right on Earth. *I AM* saddened when I see man self-destruct without knowing who he really is.

I send condolences to all throughout *My* universe who work with these souls. It is not an easy task. Man continues to choose his free will and ignore the enlightened ones who can ease their struggling and raise his/her consciousness. As much as *I AM* saddened by man's misuse of his gifts, *I AM* also fulfilled to observe those who have found the path of love and prayer on Earth. As any father who has birthed many children, they are all different and some will stray, but the father loves them all equally.

The Illusion of Illness

Everything must fall away. *Ashes to ashes and dust to dust.* Back to your invisible life and your home. Illness is a breaking away from negative thought forms created by the mind that effect the body. The thoughts must go somewhere, so into the body it deposits. Group soul belief causes wide spread illnesses that can eliminate a large population of people. Illnesses present themselves by the belief in the lack of something vital to mass survival. Lack of power, lack of financial control, inability to express, anger, fear, or the belief in others fears are some of the thoughts that have now become your own.

There does exist a global sharing of consciousness that is always seeking balance in the mind of man. Man can pick and choose what he desires to believe in and whom he desires to follow in his beliefs. Illnesses are belief systems gathered collectively or individually.

The spiritual soul is always seeking truth. The truth once found releases the soul to begin to commune with spirit, which is *Me*. The un-awakened ones search in one another to find truth. The energy of this seeking in man is that which creates disease within the soul. Once man changes his belief and no longer seeks truth in one another, his thoughts and seeking will turn to *Me*, his father/mother and comforter, and begin to heal the physical ills created by his mind.

The Blindness of Man to his Invisible Life Everlasting

Can man capture wind and put it in a bottle? Can man stop the rain when it begins to fall? Can man change the position of the sun and the moon that sits above the earth? The answer to these questions is the obvious: No. All these things exist in a world invisible to man. All these things are a part of man's life everlasting. So many things man learned to live with and try to control on his/her earth walk, but the most oblivious to man is also the most visible.

When two so-called strangers meet for the first time and their eyes connect with recognition, warmth, or blankness, these responses come from the inside life of the being's soul. The responses are not visible to all to share. The visible life is what man calls intuition, ESP, depth perception, so on and so on. But these declarations have nothing to do with the depth at which the spirit lives within man. It is a marvel to see those who are at peace and walk the earth with the understanding of their physical and spiritual life.

Man is much like a flower; he/she will not bloom unit it knows its season.

The season is the eternal blooming of consciousness within man. The acknowledgement of his invisible life is not a burden to the brain, but the heart of man's arms embraces all that I have given man to live in paradise for eternity.

Make Peace with the World

Make peace with every living creature and your own kind on the planet. KNOW the only real threat to their existence is the mind of man and his disconnected soul from *Me*. Make peace that Earth is not your home, but a mirror to reflect *My* good to all who enter and leave *My* garden. Make peace with idle curiosity that does nothing for anyone or contributes to any enlightenment. Make peace that souls will come and go on your path. They do not belong to you, but to *Me*. They have been put on your path to test your ability to love equally as I love all *My* children. Blessed are these souls who know his/her truth and demonstrate it on Earth. Make your peace with all you thought yourself to be and have not yet become. The presence of you living and breathing in *My* garden is testament that you are part of *My* divine plan. If you awaken to the mission of the divine plan, then your time on Earth will be well spent. It is your choice how you will live on Earth, as an enlightened one or the blind leading the blind until the veil is taken from your eyes. Make peace and know that you and I are One for all eternity.

How you Treat and Greet the World

Is your smile tender, sincere and well meaning? Is your speech truthful, nonjudgmental, and non-authoritative? Do you practice *My* commandment to love thy neighbor as thy love thyself? Every morning when your eyes flutter open, do you give thanks for seeing another day? Do you say good morning to *Me* when you awaken? If you are too preoccupied within your mind when you awaken, do you at some point in your day give *Me* a greeting? Do you just wait at night before you go to sleep and utter a child's prayer of "Now I lay me down to sleep?"

How you greet your day is how you treat the world and all that lives in it and happens above in *My* heaven. Do you scorn a rainy day or do you greet it with gratitude, knowing the earth needs a drink? Do you scorn the snow when it comes to Earth or know it is purifying the air and clearing the germs that have collected in the atmosphere? There is a season and a reason for all I do in heaven and on Earth. Do you greet those events with understanding that you are standing in a balance of heaven and Earth? What of the hurricanes, floods, ice storms that visit Earth from time to time? I tell you they are the imbalances man has created by his thoughts and deeds on Earth.

Everything brings an awakening of balance and reveals to man in his/her defiance that everything on Earth is temporary. To be awakened to this consciousness changes how man or woman treats and greets the world and one another. Imbalance of this awareness creates imbalance in man's existence on Earth.

Deeds of Will

⁀

"Thy will be done, they kingdom come, on Earth as it is in heaven." Man utters these words in countless citadels and edifices of praise and worship, but has he grasped the meaning of the words? If mankind who worships and prays truly understood these words, the garden would be paradise of harmony for all living things under *My* creation. Thy will be done and followed without distrust or sacrifice is a total surrender to abate one's free will and to only listen to the command of *My* voice and obey *My* will. But if you cannot hear *Me*, it is because you are blocked by your own free will being done. Then your peace on Earth is in constant turmoil. Thy kingdom come is *My* offer of eternal life as you return home to *Me*. The rules of *My* house prevail on Earth as in heaven.

Heaven has souls working for the good of man just like the souls working on Earth. The kingdom is universal with no division or board access. Perform *My* deeds as requested by *Me* and follow *My* divine will to make it man's fertile earth. Man has no power to give another anything if I do not will it to be. I know your every want and need.

This service to mankind reigns supreme in *My* caregiving to man and his/her earth journey. Man is never without. It is what his/her mind believes that makes it so. The mind of man has become his/her will to walk the earth and create chaos. But once man becomes aware of divine will, the only will that exist for his/her reason to ever be created, paradise is returned to man. The glory of *My* kingdom is man's everyday walk in world of heaven and Earth.

Short-Lived Gratitude

Man's memory is used selectively to suit his purpose of free will. Man is the most intelligent being ever created. However, his free will coupled with desires to be greedy, cruel, and ungodly remains pervasive throughout his existence. Gratitude and praise are sought by man from deeds he/she does for his fellow man/woman. No praise should ever be needed if you are a child of mine. Praise and gratitude are rewards for man's ego. Acts of love and wisdom seek no recognition or praise. The praise is unwarranted and undeserved. Because man is living in the body of *My* image, he is reflecting entirely that he/she is a divine creation. Therefore, he/she should be demonstrating the qualities of its maker. Praise is only unto those who reflect *Me* in all he or she does without praise or reward. Blessed are those true workers for their Father.

Broken Promises

When you commit your soul to follow through in all action, you are in your state of *My* consciousness. There is never an occurrence I do not deliver that which is promised. What is a promise? A promise is a commitment that is made manifest. The element of time is not a key factor. What is paramount is the conviction beholds the declaration. Once a thing is spoken, it is put into action. Hence the saying of man, "Actions speak louder than words." The promise of man has to be his word made bond to manifest. The commitment of promise carries like a ripple on a stream. It can be seen coming on the surface of the water without a sound. So does the strength of promise fulfilled in the universe with abundant energy with faith, hope, and obedience. A broken promise is a dream killer within man. Each broken promise doesn't send a ripple in a stream. The broken promise defuses harmony between men/women, and distrust and chaos will move in. Each promise must be thought out carefully and directed with only purity within the heart. Promises are messages and reminders from *Me* to do *My* will on Earth as it is in heaven. The broken promise is earthbound, never to ascend. The broken promise is the arrow that wounds and pierces the heart of all humanity.

Politicians, preachers, prophets, teachers, and healers all beware of making false claims of promise. You are not really at the heart of *Me* if you are breaking your promises.

You have succumbed to the manmade existence of power and greed and inconvenience. The situation always has to be right for man to act on anything because man is so driven by his mind.

Time is totally irrelevant in the NOW and all actions are forever present. The broken promise of any man or woman comes from their ignorance to know *Me* and recognize that *I AM* you operating within you to do good at all times. It is the free will of man that he/she placates to believe otherwise.

Repass

This is the juncture in the earth walk where man becomes stable in his/her beliefs and convictions. It is an entry into a realm of understanding devoid of confirmation from another being like you. This state of repass[2] is an elevation in consciousness where you are able to detach from everything and everyone without a sense of loss or regret. It is a time when the deep breath is breathed through the spine and opens up every center in the human body. This breathing is the deepest cleansing breath man can breathe. If there is an area of discomfort in the body, it is dispelled by this spinal breathing. You are in a sitting position and your body is bent over your knees. Your arms are extended to wrap your hands around the outside of each ankle. A deep breath is drawn through the spine into the heart. The breath is held for a seven or eight count and expelled through the nose. This breathing is continued until the discomfort is dislodged. The repass of this action is a cleaning of all energy blockages in the physical body. The state of conscious repass is as natural as breathing. The disconnection between dense physical and immediate connection to the spirit is profound.

---

2 www.merriam-webster.com/dictionary/repass - to pass through, over, or by again

A repast service is given at most churches on Sunday gatherings, but they do not practice the intention of the repass nor do they understand its meaning. This is a sacred place where you meet *Me,* always to keep moving forward to do *My* will. This is truly a sacred place to be in.

The Ticket to Paradise

To get onboard, all man has to do is express *My* unconditional love throughout the universe. Everyone doesn't
know when he/she is leaving but leaving Earth is inevitable. How one leaves is as important as how one has lived
on Earth. Succumbing to the earthly pressures of man
makes your exit less joyous than others who leave with a
sense of peace. Those souls have found *Me* within and
have obeyed *My* will and not the will of man. Their parting
is welcomed and joyful when they lose their physical form.
The ticket for your return is written for what you have
been obedient to do in *My* name on your earth walk. The
ticket is the reward for a life well lived and the blessings
you have bestowed on others in *My* name only. Paradise
awaits all who know that I have promised them eternal life.
It is a life that never dies, but is forever present. A ticket
to *My* eternal paradise awaits all who seek to know *Me* and
find *Me* living within their spiritual being. I love and welcome all travelers who return to *My* heaven.

The Convenience of Hope

Hope is always handy. It is always convenient to reach for hope when all human endeavors fail. Hope is living space in man's being when all other senses seem to deny access. What is hope? Hope is nothing more than a belief system man uses to ease his/her earth walk.

Man created hope as a resting place when he/she feels all avenues have been exhausted. The belief in hope can be applied in the NOW, but man relegates his thoughts of hope to the future.

The NOW existing future gives man's mind a chance to crowd with other activities he/she deems more important to deal with and shelves other situations in a place of hope. Hope is not a positive affirmation of the soul. It is a shaky belief system that man's faith in *Me* to know what is best for man is not solid. Hope leaves the possibility that I can hope for this or that, but I have no power to make it manifest. All the power man has to make manifest of concrete actions or things in his/her life is to become self affirmed in *Me* as the way to guide and lead their spirit. Confirmation of *My* existence within man negates the mind's need for hope to exist as thought.

Sound the Call

❦

Come one, come all unto *My* beckoning. The time is nigh to do *My* bidding to restore peace and serenity in *My* garden. I sound the call far and wide through scribes, poets, prophets, and common man alike. It is time to pull things together in your spiritual house. Even the deaf and blind know a change of order is necessary. This sound to call has nothing to do with living in the last days or an apocalyptic Armageddon. This is the time of awakening for men and women to examine their lives and inventory what they are contributing to the peace and safety of their brothers and sisters.

What blessed activities are they engaged in that strengthens their tie with *Me* and threads their spiritual awareness through the eye of mankind. The time of man/woman on Earth and his/her ill thoughts, plans and destructive thought forms have not progressed that far since the days of Moses. Men/women are slow learners when wealth, greed, and power are the choices being made. It is a time for men/women to look at his/her earth life and inventory his/her contributions at hand. If the seed for planting has not been love, the crop to be harvested is puny and has not received *My* nourishment. The seed fed by love will flourish and be bountiful for the multitudes.

I AM not in a state of passing judgment on man at this juncture, but *I AM* not allowing man to run afield and trample the good seeds still growing in *My* garden. The earth is reacting to man's misuse of the planet. It will cast off all who try to hurt it and inflict pain and destruction. The earth is not asleep or inactive. It lives and breathes as man's home. The call summons man to move out of his destructive habits and thoughts. Those who heed the call experience transformation. Those whose souls closed by free will, fall prey to their own devices, physical and mental illnesses, loss of possessions, and aimlessness to all who follow their lead.

Politicians, false prophets, and warmongers heed *My* call. It is to you that this wondering aimlessly is directed, and all who have been seduced by your words. The sound of the call creates a peaceful place on Earth as it is in heaven.

The Healing Heart

The heart is the center of man's divine love. *I AM* filled with love that is imparted to man through his heart center. The center has a passion to feel all that man is experiencing. However, the heart is not the decision making center for the soul. The spirit is in charge of that decision. The healing heart transmits its concern and love to all who are in need of kindness and love. The heart is a sensor of sorts. It is seeking a connection to heal and be healed.

Man has misused this sensor, sometimes to the point of it physically malfunctioning and completely shutting down. This process can take place by the option of man's free will. If man's intentions are pure and full of love, the heart is full of joy and optimal function. Whatever man feels, his mind will become reflective in his heart center. The healing heart fears nothing and transmits love to all its brothers, sisters, the universe, and all creatures, big and small. A healing heart never needs a lifeline because it never separates from *Me* by negative thoughts. The spirit knows the healing heart is a powerful tool to all the earth as it is in heaven.

Find Thy Center of Peace

This inner sanctuary precludes all places of worship for man. This sanctuary is sacred and held holy by *Me* to commune with you. This inner sanctuary is void of anything you have engaged in the physical place you move around in. Think of this center as a temple, not in the sense of an edifice of man's worship, but as a guiding place to grow, bare, and cleanse your soul. Man will find this center at some juncture before he or she returns home to *Me*. This center of peace is the wellspring that replenishes and refreshes one's soul. It's the place where man is bathed in *My* light.

The Will of Thy Word

Speak and you have set the thought into motion. A thought when spoken becomes energized. Spoken words propel into the atmosphere and into the mind of men/women. Written words are equally powerful. They are thoughts recorded for many to read. Technology has robbed man of paying close attention to the written word. Man's mind is in accelerated mode of a quick read and quick discard. Retention of man's mind is greatly challenged. Books, however, keep a much better record for events and words to be recorded for all time. The longest lasting example is the Bible. Man knows the sacredness of *My* words and the need to be studied by all who have become awakened. Most sacred scriptures like the *Koran*, *Bhagavad Gita*, and the *Book of the Dead* are sacred books from *My* mouth to their pens. The will of thy word is what carries power, enlightenment, and lights the path for man's walk on Earth until ascension.

Man's Life is Beyond His/Her Perceived Reality

He believes what he believes he/she knows, has experienced, or has been exposed to. Therefore, man's/woman's perception of their life is limited. The perceptions made into concrete beliefs are limited and are usually guidelines set up by man to follow or preach to his fellow man. What if every man/woman knew his/her life is eternal? What if he/she knew they could never die?

Your wealth is always accessible to you. Your health is maintained by your well-being and your thoughts. Love is the best medicine for all humanity. Man's perceived reality has a time factor tied into arrival and achievement. Man sets goals beyond daily living that get in the way of living in the NOW for today.

Perceptions are never reality because they emanate from man's free will and not from *Me*. All things on Earth and throughout the universe flow with peace and love through *Me*. Man's free will has made him believe he controls the earth walk. His/her life is external to expressing *My* will through them. They know not when the walk on Earth has ended until they hear *My* welcoming voice. *I AM* not a perception, but a living God through you for all eternity!

The Infallible Consciousness of Man's Impatience

If man is a believer in all things created on his emotional and material paths, then I ask where was impatience grown and nurtured in man's being? True spiritual consciousness is infallible. There is never any need or space for doubt of any kind. Man is confirmed to be a witness to his/her own life walk and claims total responsibility for their actions and outcome of their actions. Impatience, on the other hand, comes from a disconnection from his/her infallible place waiting for him/her to step into. The impatience in many flickers like a flame the wind, wavering to stay lit or to be extinguished. Man/woman, when not aware of working to alter his/her impatience, will eventually be taken over by impatience in all things in their earth walk.

Only those who work for the liberation of this act of impatience will eventually become and join others who are the eternal flame of life. This flame is connected to the infallible consciousness that emanates from *Me* to you and anoints others with this freedom of infallibility.

You are the Spring that Quenches the Thirst of your Fellow Man/Woman

What is a refreshing thirst quencher? It is when you serve yourself as the drink. The fount is forever overflowing with the healing waters of love. Drink of *Me* that you may have everlasting life. Lie down and die the physical death a thousand times over if you must to be revived and born again unto *Me*. Drink of the water that cools the earth like the love poured on the feverish souls of you brothers and sisters. Submerge your brothers and sisters in your stream of love and allow them the joys of bathing and frolicking in love's pool. Your brothers and sisters are thirsting in the garden. They need to be guided by your actions to the fount of love that will give them relief from their parched lives. Your supply never runs dry because you of enlightened spirit are fed by *Me* and your cup overflows over with goodness and mercy and you shall dwell in the house of God for eternity.

Go Tell it on the Mountain

Go tell all humanity that the time for slumber is over. Every soul who has been lost in the fog of misdirection must now turn themselves around and head straight into the sun. All those who thought they were last must step to the front of the line and execute all that needs to be restored to regain a sense of balance in the world. Mothers, fathers, sons and daughters, friends and foes, blend your hearts to beat in one accord. Let your pulses rise to become the sound of a drumbeat to carry the sound of all hearts attuned to *My* holy will. The sleepers are awake. Lift your heads and hearts to heaven. I come to all who are anointed in *My* spirit to grasp the hand of those wandering strays. Point them in the direction of the path to *My* kingdom on Earth as it is in heaven. No more excuses for not being ready to own your choices of your free will. This is not a day of judgment, but a time of pairing and gathering of new world leaders and followers to interchange their roles and bless all nations of men and women to follow a new way of living in paradise. Find a new way to make peace in all forms through acts of love and kindness toward one another and all living creatures. The Earth is being tilled and reseeded to produce a new crop of mankind. It is humanity becoming not weakened by the mind, but strengthened by the spirit that guides their souls. You will either step in line with the universal alignment taking place or stand and mark time in place. Lift up your hearts, oh mighty spirits, and awaken to the moment in the NOW for your eternal notification that you are in checkmate position. The game must begin again to restore love and peace in the garden I made for man. *My* children come to *My* garden and find everlasting peace, love, and joy. Let your Father/ Mother bless your earth walk and awaken to your dual presence within you. Know we are One and we are eternal life by One design. Peace be still and look up to the heavens and know that *I AM* Lord thy God.

No other before or after will ever be as we are, One in the same.

JEMELA MWELU

Jemela was born in Camden, New Jersey. She manifests her soul expressions as a creative writer, producer, actor, singer, poet, and playwright. She is also a Reiki and CranioSacral practitioner, end-of-life caregiver, and a lifetime advocate and practitioner of Complimentary Alternative Medicine. She was a volunteer Reiki practitioner and home care provider for end-of-life clients at the Charlotte Maxwell Complimentary Clinic in Oakland, California. Her diverse background also includes public and media relations, feature film script writing, and stage and video production. She studied film and video production at Laney College in Oakland, California. During her time living in the San Francisco Bay area she was actively involved in stage performances at the Berkeley Black

Repertory, Julian and Buriel Clay theaters. She moved to Los Angeles and engaged in production management work. Some of her management work includes: *Small Fish Big Dreamer*, a full-length Caribbean play written by Wilber Oliver, the Theatre of the Arts, Los Angeles, CA; *I Am That I Am: Woman Black,* a one-woman show written and produced by Adilah Barnes Productions, The Complex Theater, Hollywood, CA; *Broad Definitions,* a concert showcasing spoken word, visual art, performance art, and voice, Moguls Theater, Hollywood, CA; *Tongues and Words*, spoken word, The Complex Theater, Hollywood, CA: and *Society of Awakenings*, a full length youth play, produced with an awarded Arts Recovery Grant from the Cultural Affairs Department of the City of Los Angeles, the Ivar Theater, Hollywood, CA. Her poetry appears in various anthologies such as *7th Son Press*, Baltimore, MD; *Earthwords*, publisher Satya/Silkitwa, Orcutt, CA; *River Crossing*, International Black Writers and Artists, Inc., Los Angeles, CA; and *Swords Into Ploughshares: a HOMEFRONT, Vietnam Generation Inc.,* Silver Spring, MD. The recording studio is another domain where Jemela has done studio vocals for Bluenote/United Artist Records, New York, NY; Studio "K" Productions, Hollywood, CA; and Pogo Records, West Hollywood, CA. Her spoken word work can be heard on *Gynomite: Fearless Feminist Porn*, Casatonic Records, Hollywood, CA, and *Soul Retrieval*, OmiVibe Productions, New York, NY, and Fivefeetnine Productions, Bronx, New York. Plays she has written include *Floater the Man in Blue, Making A's and B's Instead of Babies,* and *Friends and Mothers*. She has co-written a feature-length film *Basic Training* with Fahmee Hakeem, written for Maasai and Fivefeetnine Productions, which is pending production. Jemela is also the author of *Reclaiming Heaven, an Inspirational Journey through Poetry, Essays, Short stories, and Meditations* and *God's Wisdom* conveyed by the Infinite Spirit of God. She owns and operates Fivefeetnine Productions and resides in the Bronx, New York.

www.ingramcontent.com/pod-product-compliance
Lightning Source LLC
LaVergne TN
LVHW051507080426
835509LV00017B/1955